Awakening The Internal

How to Become a Man of Strength and Freedom

Ken Curry, LMFT

ISBN: 0692594752
ISBN-13: 978-0692594759 (Solid Man)

AWAKENING THE INTERNAL

Pillar One

HOW TO BECOME A MAN OF STRENGTH AND FREEDOM

KEN CURRY LMFT

DEDICATION

This one is for Colleen

ACKNOWLEDGMENTS

Thanks to my family who has been alongside me as I have developed this process. You have seen my struggles and personal development in real time right in front of you. Your feedback and support has been so important to me.

Thanks to the men of my groups. Your courage and ability to rise to all the challenges that I have given you will always be an inspiration. You have been the benefactors of this process and my appreciation goes to you for being the "guinea pigs" as this process was discovered and developed.

CONTENTS

PREFACE

Welcome to the Solid Man Process. Presently our world is experiencing a significant loss. Something vital is missing for the health and structure of our world. Even though you may not recognize what it is, you have felt this loss on a personal level. It's probably why you're reading this.

For decades now, what we believe about men and the role of men in family and society has been questioned. While initially this scrutiny was necessary, it has resulted in enormous changes about what we believe about the value of men. Because of this, you may have wondered about your own value or questioned whether it is even good to be a man.

How men interact with and influence the world has been under the microscope. The result has been confusion and uncertainty about the role of men. Because of this turmoil, many men have lost the good, strong core of their manhood.

The Solid Man Process is designed to help men reclaim that center, so the entire world can experience good, positive masculinity.

This experience develops five significant aspects in your life which builds a core of strength and freedom. This is the Pillar One of a Solid Man; Awakening the Internal.

There are two parts to this first Pillar; Part One - The Problem; The Externally Referenced Life and then Part Two - The Solution; Awakening the Internal. There are interactive questions and challenges throughout this book. You can read this however you want; with a quick first read and then work through the questions and challenges or dig in deep from the start, you make the call.

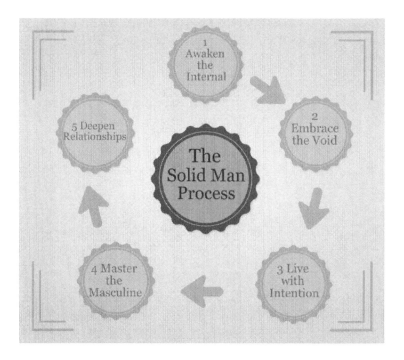

Pillar One is designed so you can develop an internally referenced life to become awake and alive in your life. This is essential work in order for you to develop your strength and to live in freedom.

Usually men's "work" tries to fix what's wrong with you. With this process, we will release what is right about you. Some men think something in our core is our enemy that needs to be reined in. So we fight ourselves as though we are our own enemy. In this process, we will let go of that fight, eliminate self-attack and listen to the real challenges that being a man gives us.

This process will uncover a deeper framework within you and help you develop a set of skills and practices designed for change. It is a holistic approach which respects the integration of body, heart, spirit and community.

Our problems are a doorway into what really needs attention. If we allow them to, they will take us to something deeper and important. Whatever that thing is, it is on the other side of the threshold calling for our attention. This process invites us into that unknown place so we can restore our lives.

Struggles are a great teacher that is asking us to learn what we need to learn about ourselves. Too many of us consider anger, anxiety, sex drive and our internal struggles to be the worst parts of us. So we take a pill, or limit ourselves and beat ourselves into submission.

Until we learn that our challenges are here to teach us and until we listen and learn those lessons we will keep recycling back to our problems since nothing is ever resolved.

This process is not about those symptoms; porn, anxiety, anger, broken relationships or whatever is troubling you. It is about considering the places in life where the action really is; your story, your identity, your family of origin, your sexuality, your purpose, your relationships, spirituality and beliefs, your interaction with community and all arenas of your life.

You've probably found yourself in endless cycles of trying to fix stuff because you've not considered the deeper areas of life like resentments, shame, unfinished relational business or repressing your needs or passions. As you take care of the deeper stuff you will be surprised how the endless cycles subside dramatically.

Be humble, be a student, decipher the lessons that are there to teach you. There is an unseen wisdom behind your internal process. It will all make sense. You will discover the hidden messages. Wisdom is calling out for your attention from deep within you.

There are no shortcuts. Life is now insisting that you to wake up and do the work. In every challenge there is a roadmap through that challenge and into the truth. Let your own wisdom find it.

The Solid Man Process is about empowering every man. The more we become personally empowered the more we reach our potential. What goes on in our heart, mind and spirit has a potent impact on all aspects of our life. When we become who we are meant to be, our life begins to become the greatest version of what it was meant to be.

As you read the following pages, you will find yourself reacting to different ideas. Some things will resonate with you deeply and other ideas will bristle against something. Regardless, as much as you can, stay with the process and question everything you react to.

Some of these ideas may go against what you've been told throughout your life. Challenge everything; what you've been taught in life and even what you are being told here. Allow your own wisdom and heart to integrate truth with the core of who you are, who you know you really are.

If the way you are moving through life right now is working for you, then disregard what I have to say. You are probably already living from many of these principles already. So keep on in the life you have with passion and intent.

This journey is most effective when done with other men. Invite and gather a few men to go through this journey with you. Since this is a lifetime process, you'll need to be ready to learn, listen and interact with other men.

As you work through this process, it is important to be open as possible; conscious and aware of what you are feeling and thinking. Processing deep things and checking in with yourself will be awkward at first. So checking in with other men may seem really awkward as well. But soon you will regret not having men with you all along.

I have been studying the world of men and where we find ourselves at this pivotal time in history. I process this material with other men on a daily basis. A great conversation is growing and I anticipate a strong resurgence of men challenging one another to gain confidence in being good, solid men. In my reading, three authors stand out to me as I developed this work; Dr. Robert Glover, John Eldredge and Dr. Brené Brown.

If you have read anything from Glover or experienced any of his courses, you will see Dr. Glover's influence throughout my writing. The ideas in his book _No More Mr. Nice Guy_ was one thing that started me developing this process. He opened up concepts that changed the pathway of my life as he has for many of you. My hope is that as he has opened up so many men to the challenge of a significant problem, my work will continue to create additional solutions to the problem he addresses.

Two of Eldredge's books have influenced me here as well; _Wild at Heart_ and _Waking the Dead_. _Wild at Heart_ long ago gave me permission to challenge the status quo in my life and _Waking the Dead_ challenged me to consider the idea that my heart is good. Creating a positive view of your internal core is a huge concept in this work.

Dr. Brené Brown has been influential because this work wrestles often with shame and vulnerability. These have been topics she dives into in her talks and books. To get more of a taste of what she has to say, listen to her Ted talks or read one of her books.

Along with these three, there have been many influences in my journey. Some of these have been friends, some family and some highly difficult circumstances. It has been a demanding pathway with victories and defeat.

I suppose this is just how it will be for everyone, becoming a Solid Man is a long journey of learning, change and growth. You will encounter pitfalls, obstacles, and challenges of all kinds.

In this book you will see my personal notes in italics, like this. From the challenges in my life and from my journey this process has developed. I recognize many places where I could have quit, but for some reason I have stayed with it. In a sense, this work reflects my story. And since I am a regular man as you are, I am certain this is your story as well. My hope is that these notes from my journey will give you some clarity and waypoints for orientation as you go through life. Just like me, your journey will take time, persistence and energy. Stay with the process, be patient, it is worth it.

Reflection Questions

At the end of each section you will find questions designed to help get some movement in your life. It is essential that you take time to ponder each question so you can begin to develop changes you need. Many people find that journaling helps things sink in, so grab a notebook and write out your answers. You will also find a more concise set of questions after Part One and Part Two designed for you to use to present to your group.

What are ways you have tried to fix the problems in your life that haven't worked?

What resistance do you have to the idea of inviting other men? Why do you think this is?

Solid Challenges

At the end of each chapter there is a "Solid Challenge". These will take more effort, but are essential in the journey to complete the shifts you need. Pillar One is designed so you can develop an internally referenced life to become awake and alive in your life. This is essential work in order for you to develop your strength and to live in freedom.

It is important to take the time to consider the questions and then write your answers down. Often men will try to bypass the process and get to fixing the problem. Stay in the process and take the time this needs, Here's Solid Challenge #1.

Solid Challenge #1: Goals

Write down what you hope to accomplish with the Solid Man Process.

What were the events leading you to even starting to read this?

What are your goals, things that you want to happen in your life?

What is it that you want in your life that you are missing?

Imagine the best possible outcome you can think of, write that down. Think of your relationships, work, spiritually, health, lifestyle, purpose, and any other category that is important to you.

INTRODUCTION

The Call

You are reading this because something has started to awaken in your life. Maybe it is just time for a change. Maybe you have been caught in a cycle of unhealthy behavior that you know must end. Maybe someone gave you an ultimatum to get stuff fixed. The message could have been from a book or a challenge from a friend who is getting his shit together.

Whatever and wherever the call to change came from, it is time to rise to the challenge and change the trajectory of your life. It is time to step over the threshold into a completely different way of living. It is a call to adventure, to something alive and real.

For me the call to something bigger first came from a deep stirring inside me. I began to experience huge incongruity between what the culture was saying and expecting of me as a man and what my heart or my soul was telling me about myself.

There were two completely different messages about who I was and what a man is. I began to discover that there has been a full court press pushing me and all men into a narrative about how we needed to act and what we needed to believe about ourselves. But even with that pressure, the instinctive truth buried in my soul began to rise up and be identified.

Many men have felt that same deep stirring and are beginning to talk about it. The discussion about the place we find ourselves is a diverse dialogue, often called the "manosphere". It may be that some of these voices have been what has initiated your entrance into awareness.

In the manosphere, this awareness is often equated to the challenge that Neo was given by Morpheus in *The Matrix*. The challenge was to make a choice to take the blue pill or to take the red pill. It is true for you here as well, if you keep on in your "blue pill" ways you will continue to live in a fog of expectation, enslaved to the ways the culture has defined you.

If you take the "red pill" your eyes will begin to be opened to the realities about how you've been trained and duped to keep a machine going. That awareness will be followed by the challenge to live from the deep truths that exist within your being to begin to master living your own life.

The Challenge

As you engage in developing more awareness and change, you will experience resistance and obstacles. You will be tested in ways you never imagined. Your woman will test to see if this is real, if you are really solid and secure for her.

Your family and friends will push you to get back into your old posture. The culture will be relentless to cram you back into your place. People you thought were on your side will betray you because you are not playing the expected role.

Expect there to be guardians keeping the status quo. They are standing at the threshold like they always have been, keeping you from experiencing your true life. Whatever the shape they take, they will be fearful to you. Face them with courage and keep moving ahead.

This is all to be expected, your relationships are where your training happens in your journey. This is where you will put to practice what you are learning.

⮧ **Your relationships are your proving grounds.**

Finding resilience with the obstacles and resistance is a powerful part of gaining mastery of your own life. That which seems to thwart you will actually become the force that builds your solidness.

You will falter, but you will learn. Everything in your life will become an opportunity to gain feedback so you can gain mastery. You will begin to taste freedom and that taste will drive you to stay strong and overcome.

Some of you will reject these ideas and fall back into the Blue Pill life. But those of you with courage will begin to thrive like you never thought possible.

Mentors

Use all the resources that are available as you go through the process of regaining your heart. My voice is just one of many that will guide you toward the life for which you have been designed. Read, listen, observe and talk about this with as many men as you can.

Find mentors who will guide you in getting your heart and soul back. There are podcasts, books, retreats, blogs all designed to move you to a different space in your life. Use the ones that resonate with the truths that you are discovering about yourself.

Hire a counselor or coach who will move you along the path. Surround yourself with good men who guide you well. Take this journey together. This will take time, energy, focus and money. Make a significant investment in you.

Narrative

Up to this point in your life you have settled into a narrative about who you are and what your life is all about. A narrative is a story or account of events, experiences, whether true or fictitious. You have been told various stories about your life and whether you are acceptable or not.

> ◌ **Your narrative is yours; this is your story, no one else's.**

Part of this journey is to discover the true narrative of your life. You will need to look deeply into the story you have been told about who you really are and what everyone else may have told you to believe. Reclaiming your story is essential in order to get your life where you want it to be.

Reject messages that don't move you toward freedom. Challenge the messages you have received that at the time you thought were truth. Keep a keen eye for false narratives or ideas that are designed to keep you believing lies about yourself. To find the true narrative you'll need to question everything you have held true about yourself.

I am certain the Solid Man process will get you moving toward what you want in life, but it is just a part of what you need. Gather your men, read the books and blogs and allow your relationships to test your solidness. Dig in and enjoy the process.

> ☞ **When I became a man, I put the ways of childhood behind me.** – **Apostle Paul**

Reflection Questions

How have you felt the call to be different or to reclaim something in you that seems lost?

Where did the call come from? How did you start to hear it?

What have you learned already about yourself and what is wrong with men? Where have you been learning things?

Go online and start searching the "manosphere" for blogs and see what comes up and catches your attention. What do you see?

In what ways does it feel like your story has been hi-jacked by someone else, as if someone else is running things?

How does the narrative you've been told about you, fit with what you know about you to be true from your core, or not?

In what ways have you been living an oblivious (Blue-Pill) life?

Solid Challenge #2: Mt. Rushmore

It is time to build your Mt. Rushmore.

We need other men in our lives in order to gain strength, be accountable, deal with our BS and to have fun. Other men are absolutely essential to live a Solid life, there is no other option.

MLB Manager Clint Hurdle uses the analogy of having your own personal Mount Rushmore; at least four good, solid men who with you in the journey of life. When you think of your Mt. Rushmore you will see their faces in stone and can list their names.

You need at least four men who know your story, know your dirty laundry, know your struggles, know you and your family and have absolute permission to talk about any issue of life in reciprocal fashion. It is necessary to be in contact often. Guys night out once a month would work, but hunting once in the Fall is not enough.

This isn't about just getting together to bemoan life, but having fun in life and passion, supporting when difficult things come up and walking through the ups and downs of life in real time. Most men have neglected this area of life. We may have one or two friends who we do things with every once in a while, but never veer from sports, politics or any other shallow topic. Men who struggle with porn, substance abuse, anger and other problems rarely have good, strong male relationships.

Jim Rohn said, "You are the average of the five people you spend the most time with." Take this into consideration as you choose the men in your tribe, community, crew or whatever you call it. This is essential as you grow into the man you are.

Another perspective is from the movie/documentary **_Five Friends_**. Check it out at http://fivefriendsmovie.com/

Write down the list of potential Rushmore men. Who do you admire? Who is already there? Who could possibly one of your men?

Now list them in order of potential. If they are already on your Mt. Rushmore list them first.

Now plan how you will start to make it happen. Either talk to them about this concept and see if they are interested, or just start getting together. Write your plan.

How can you invite them to be with you, together going through the Solid Man Process?

Write down the list of potential mentors.

Write down five action steps to get them to be with you in your journey.

PART ONE; THE EXTERNALLY REFERENCED LIFE

None are more hopelessly enslaved than those who falsely believe they are free.   **- Johann Wolfgang von Goethe**

This first part is a gut check. It is going to require that you look deeply into how you've developed the way that you relate to your world. You will need to be honest and open about the state of your life right now. With courage face the resistance you experience as you listen to these words and ask yourself the follow-up questions from the workbook.

The Solid Man Process is about mastering the art of fully and freely being good at being a man. Being a man is about living with freedom, strength, courage and love. Men want to live with significant personal power and self-control as we make a positive influence in our world. Let's have a look at why we don't always live like that.

I have always struggled through life in a number of ways with self-confidence, my sexuality and anger. While there are a number of reasons for this, I am about to share with you the core reason these problems were in my life. Listen closely to how your heart interacts with this stuff, that is the key to your transformation.

1 THE PROBLEM DEFINED

Even though men are very hesitant to declare or even recognize it, we experience many difficulties in life. The problems we face on a daily basis manifest in various ways unique to each man.

Here is a list of some of what our troubles often look like. As you read this list consider what rings true for you. This is a long list, so take your time. Read each one out loud and mark the ones you have experienced.

- lacking confidence, personal power, purpose or meaning

- fear based living, worry or anxiety

- confusion about manhood or masculinity

- sexual issues like performance, porn or compulsivity

- emotional issues like anger, depression, or bottling stuff up

- being emotionally unavailable to self and others

- living in your head and relying only on logic

- relational disruptions in your closest relationships

- having a posture of aggression, intimidation or abuse

- spiritual disconnections or loss of moral compass ✓

- poor decision making, procrastination or being stuck ✓

- escaping to compartmentalizing, disengagement or withdrawal ✓

- various addictions, self-medicating or distractions ✓

- inability to transition fully from boyhood to manhood ✓

- lack of focus, presence and leadership ✓

- being unreliable or not trustworthy

- passivity, frozenness and silence ✓

With every one of these problems there are consistent threads woven through the pain men experience. In this work, Awakening the Internal, we will consider the most profound thread, which is called an **"externally referenced life"**. Confronting your own externally referenced life will free you from many problems you face in your life.

I always knew something was awry with how I was living my life. I just did not have the words for it. As I became aware of the common themes about what I believed about life from different sources the words began to become clear. Over the years I was becoming aware that how I was living is what I now call the externally referenced life.

An externally referenced life exists when a man's identity and actions are determined by what others want, what would please others and what is expected of him to fit in or be acceptable. Since he is dependent on others for his identity and motivation he has lost his freedom and his vitality. This is where painful problems take root and grow like cancer.

> ➛ **The life you want is impossible if you are driven or defined by externals.**

The goal of the Solid Man Process is to become internally referenced so you can gain freedom and vitality in your life. You have been designed to live in freedom by relying on your strong internal resources. An internally referenced man is solid; moving with confidence and influencing his world with freedom, intention and purpose.

Our problem is that we have allowed our lives to have an external point of reference, living from the **outside-in**. Like sheep, we have just accepted this way of living without looking deeply at our life. You probably are experiencing life difficulties right now and this is why you are finally willing to take a strong look at the realities of your life.

I began to recognize that because of a series of events that happened between my 9th and 10th year of life that something shifted. I changed from a happy, funny, and carefree kid to an introspective and self-conscious kid who was worried about what everyone was thinking about me. I began to second-guess every move I made and everything I believed about who I was.

Awareness of the point of reference in your life will give you the ability to live your own life. You will begin to break free from habits and patterns that have held you back from being the man you want to be.

> ➔ **A man who lives an externally referenced life will NEVER be able to experience the fullness of masculinity and manhood.**

This experience is about fully and freely being alive. As you develop a strong internally referenced life and your internals are awakened to the profound realities within you, you will gain strength in life and the problems that have haunted you will release their grip on your soul.

> ➔ **The solution is to rebuild your life upon internal realities that drive us and define us; living from the inside-out.**

Since we have built the foundation of our lives upon what others think, need, expect, we have allowed ourselves to be enslaved by what everybody else wants and needs, essentially handing the reins of your life to others.

The consequences of an externally referenced life are sad since we lose connection with our True Self, who we really are at our core. Through our reliance on externals, we have developed a False Self, an imagined identity based upon what we think will be acceptable to others.

Rebuilding your solid core of integrity begins with the essential shift from externals to internals. This journey will take time, intention and patience. It will change the path of your life, forever.

What are Externals?

Most men, push-over nice guys to hyper-masculine jerks, are driven and defined by externals in their lives. "Externals" are those forces outside of yourself which you allow to define or drive your life.

Externals can either have enormous control over you or actually be a wonderful gift in your life that creates beauty, love and a deeper sense of well-being. Externals are not bad things in themselves. Problems arise when you need them to complete your identity or when externals drive your next move.

Here is a list of some examples of externals. As with the previous list, take your time, read them out loud and notice if any resonate with you. Highlight, underline or circle the ones that do.

- Our woman and those things she might give us; sex, validation, comfort, affection, more well-being, support, appreciation, etc.

- Our boss/employer and the approval and opportunities from work; promotions, titles, salary, benefits, purpose, status, etc.

- The culture at large and what is required to be a good productive citizen; keeping the infrastructure working like a man should.

- Our often confusing family of origin; systemic dynamics, fusion, rules, roles, expectations, identity, heritage, secrets, trauma, control, abuse.

- Our accomplishments, achievements or things we do to meet expectations, to get approval, what we should do, to prove our value or show our worth.

- What police, authorities and anyone who oversees our lives expects; keeping us in line and doing what is expected.

- What the academic system has taught us about reality, origins, knowledge, what's acceptable, life, worldview, getting along, etc.

- Your device with all the apps, social media and diversions that come with the technology of our day coupled with the expectations to stay connected, respond immediately and keep up with the 'next big thing'.

- The messages from religion that shape our identity, worldview and actions so we achieve the mission or vision of the church.

- Various sources of authority to which we might choose to submit like a church leader, boss, political party, a charismatic person, or someone who provides something you need.

- All our attachments to things that we think bring us life; addictions, self-medication, counterfeits, your drug of choice.

- Peer pressure, keeping up with the Joneses, materialism with all the stuff we think we need, wearing a mask, chameleon, to look acceptable.

- Consumerism and how marketing campaigns tell us what we think we need, convincing us to buy to feel good, complete or whole.

- Groups (political, religious, sports, academic, gangs, clubs, social, cliques, etc.) that require a certain way of being in order to fit in or belong.

- Totalitarian, oppressive governments or cults where you are not free to believe, to speak or to act freely and if you do, you face difficult consequences.

These "externals" push into our lives expecting us to submit our soul in order to gain belonging or to remain acceptable.

In an online course for men on Dr. Glover's website, Roger Nix lists the externals that he pursued before he was able to gain strength over them. His list includes; anxiety, alcohol, cocaine, work, success, sex, money, status, approval, being smart and entertaining, strippers, hookers, massage parlors, porn, marriage, fast cars, Harleys, a ponytail, travel, living first class, yachts, private jets, food, sugar, traditional religion, new thought religion, spirituality, cults, therapy, abstinence, celibacy, 12 steps, gadgets, pharmaceuticals, living abroad, risk and fantasy. We all have our own list like this.

Even Solomon from the Bible pursued externals to try to find meaning in life; he went after wine, women, song, money, education (philosophy), fame, power and possessions eventually describing all those pursuits as vanity.

Externals can determine what we wear, what we buy, what we collect, what we worry about, what we think about ourselves, what we are anxious about, what team we follow, what we are afraid of and what we pursue.

Externals are things where we think life comes from; "If I only had _____(blank)_____ then I would feel whole and complete."

I have succumbed to just about the entire list, but my strongest externals have been my family of origin, the church, accomplishments and what women (especially my wife) think of me. This resulted in becoming what Glover refers to as a "nice guy" who lives for the approval of others.

When men are silent, passive, anxious, distant, defensive and living from a "damned if I do, damned if I don't" posture, externals are ALWAYS in the mix. Externals are our attachments which control us throughout our lives.

➔ **When we're controlled by an external, we will never be free.**

Consider what brings up the most fear, what brings you anxiety or anger in your life. Fear, anxiety and anger are always attached to the primary externals in your life and therefore are your greatest indicators to help you discover your own set of externals.

I have always been afraid of not getting it right, this has resulted in me always trying to figure out how to live life so people accepted me. "Figuring it Out" became my way of life and my motivation.

Reference Points

Hundreds of years ago there was the debate over which point the Solar System revolved. The Geocentrics believed everything revolved around the earth. The Heliocentrics had developed evidence that the true point of reference was actually the sun.

You heard about these guys in the fifth grade; Copernicus, Galileo, the Pope, the Church, etc. Finally, it was resolved, there was a shift in reference (from the Earth to the Sun) that changed the course of astronomy and science.

➔ **If your point of reference is off, everything else in your life will be off, you will never get life right.**

You must know that you've been following a false reference point, a lie. Men in our present culture have been taught, trained and even shamed into living with an external point of reference. We have a false reference point upon which our life is centered, therefore we actually are living a "false life". The external referenced life is not real or authentic. Our true self is hidden and closed off.

It is time to reclaim the **true** reference point from which your life has been designed to live. That true reference point is your heart or your core. You have been designed to live from an inner authority.

This idea may be contrary to what you have believed, so listen if there are any personal reactions as you read this. This will give you clues about where your reference points have been.

If you are to truly live in freedom, then you must fully be free. If you are living under some sort of external authority, then you are not truly free. Your freedom only exists if you are truly free to guide and determine the direction of your own life.

✠ **Freedom can only happen with an internal point of reference.**

I always had a sense that I was not free. I was not free to be me, without the worry if I was acceptable or if I belonged. I slowly became aware of how enslaved I truly was. Experiencing freedom has been huge. Freedom is not always easy, but it is fulfilling.

The Big Lie

The externally referenced life, where externals define you and drive your life, begins with the perception that you are flawed or something is wrong with you. This is the Big Lie.

There are many traditions that believe and communicate that something is broken or something is wrong with you, therefore your struggle in life is to "rein in the wild horses" or live on the higher plane.

To live in an acceptable life we must build self-control, be disciplined, follow the rules and straighten up and fly right. We need to recognize our powerlessness, submit to a certain set of rules or surrender our lives to a power which can actually manage our mess. It seems that recovery or success in life always has to do with placing ourselves under some sort of external authority.

From the beginning of literacy there have been stories that communicate that something in manhood is broken, not acceptable for civilization or needs to be restrained. These stories about uncontrollable masculinity ranged from classics, like Enkidu from the Epic of Gilgamesh, Robert Bly's Iron John and Beauty and the Beast, to contemporary stories like Wolverine and Bruce Banner/The Hulk.

Even the story of the Frog Prince shows the encounter with the feminine as a doorway to life. He needs the kiss from a beautiful woman to become a real man.

Theological perspectives that believe something is wrong with the heart of a man have been determined pretty much by one passage in the Bible, Jeremiah 17:9; "The heart is deceitful above all things and beyond cure. Who can understand it?"

Therefore the theological belief is that if people live freely from their hearts they will fly headlong into a crazy life of sin; immorality, greed, sex, alcohol and even dancing!

These stories and ideas say there must be an external authority that tames our broken wildness; something outside of us must control us so we can make life work, live righteously or gain acceptance. The way men are is not acceptable, something must change.

Evolutionary psychology communicates this with the endless discussion about what an "Evolved Man" looks like. This conversation assumes that the way men are needs to be fixed. We must identify and eliminate masculine deficiencies so humanity can continue to progress and evolve into the future.

This progression is seen as Science Fiction stories often have an ideal image of men in the distant future as asexual beings with huge telepathic brains and very small muscles. This looks like the ideal until Vin Diesel punches them in their gigantic heads.

Whether it is theology, literature, pop-culture or science, the message is very clear; something must be restrained or changed in every man.

Somewhere, you have been told that you're born broken, not good enough or that you are not in good working order. Therefore you cannot trust your own "Internal Resources" to guide your own life. You cannot live from your own inner authority.

⮑ **Who told you that you were broken?**

Whether it is your masculinity, your heart or some other part of you, we've been told that something is broken. That message comes out in subtle and yet obvious ways. You will discover that the real problem is actually your frame of reference, not your core.

Since we can't trust our own heart, we believe we must trust other's perceptions and expectations in order to be acceptable. We end up with this false belief, "I can only trust externals if I am going to get this right."

> ☞ **The lie is this; you are broken and you must rely on externals in order to be acceptable.**

To live from the inside-out you must break the stronghold that this lie has in your life. You must develop an internal point of reference and trust that you are in good working order.

I totally bought this lie. For the longest time I believed that something was inherently wrong with me. I really thought that God had made a horrible mistake when he made me. I felt like something was deeply flawed in me. As I began to break from this belief, the kernels of the idea of the internally referenced life began to take form.

The Dilemma; Orbit or Be Rejected

Who knows how all this happened, but in the past fifty years or so, men have been trained to orbit women and please them in order to get the scraps of external validation or sex.

This was a posture that I thought was what I needed to do in order to be seen as a good man. I lived this way for many years thinking that it was not only acceptable, but required. I believed this was how a man was designed to be in his life.

Often meant in jest, messages like, "If Momma Ain't Happy, Ain't Nobody Happy" or "Happy Wife, Happy Life" reinforce what the primary job of a man is in this present culture; to please. Like a fish born into the water, we know nothing different. Many of us believe that this is what we have been born for; to please and make others happy.

> ☞ **Like sputnik, you're a satellite which has no gravity of its own, beep, beep, beeping through life.**

With those external messages that tell us we are broken, we are our own worst critic. Our self-judgments and criticisms crumble our core and mess with our identity. These messages have gone deep into us. We are unaware how deep. Many externally referenced men despise their own masculinity and sexuality. In our own shame, we have created strong judgments against our own core.

> ☞ **We can be our own worst enemy.**

Taking care of ourselves, trusting ourselves, leading and even loving ourselves has become a lost art. We actually believe that caring for ourselves or saying what we want is "selfish".

After being laid off from a job, I remember a good friend asking me what I wanted. I couldn't even answer. I was dumbfounded. I had never even asked myself that question. Asking me what I wanted was the most selfish question. I had been avoiding anything that seemed selfish. I was always asking what everybody else wanted. I see now that this idea came from misconstrued interpretations from my faith tradition, I never heard it outright, but the message was clear; attending to your self was not acceptable, it was shame.

The false narrative that masculinity is inherently bad leaves us with no option but self-judgment and shame. In order to fit in and be acceptable we have chosen to defer to externals defining who we are and driving what we do. So we live to please others, to make sure we are not seen as selfish.

So this is the dilemma; do I orbit around others trying to please them (which I hope results in getting the validation I need) or do I become a selfish A-hole who lives to please himself. These seem like our only options.

The external point of reference starts with the belief that you are broken, flawed, and unacceptable. So you compensate, trying to look good or to measure up. But the problem is that when comparing with others you never match up.

There always seems to be someone, something or someplace where you don't measure up. There is always someone smarter, better looking and funnier. We always question ourselves and lose confidence.

> ☞ **Even when your behavior is right, you'll still believe your core is wrong.**

If I believe I am broken, I will never be able to trust my core processes that give me all the information I need to make my next move in life.

There seems to be overwhelming evidence that something is wrong with me; I make bad decisions, I am stuck in poor behaviors, I keep coming back to those behaviors over and over, I can't get it right, I don't measure up. This is how evidence works when it is based on externals.

We read the writing on the wall; "Your Honor, the evidence is clear, this man has been weighed, measured, and found wanting!" We are unacceptable.

Our self-created externally referenced "identity hodge-podge" (parents, siblings, coaches, peers, bullies, teachers, co-workers, bosses, spouses, religion, culture, etc.) always fails us. We will never measure up. We will never be good enough. The evidence always says "failure".

On the contrary, driving your own life requires a solid sense of self defined from internal sources and truth about who you really are. Freedom is having the power to act, speak, or think as you want without hindrance or restraint.

Enslaved

When we rely on externals for our identity and motivation, we have voluntarily placed ourselves into "slavery" or under some external authority. We believe we must gain some sense of value or worthiness through what we achieve or what others (especially women) think about us. We have become slaves to externals when we live with an external point of reference.

➔ **We have voluntarily placed ourselves under a yoke of slavery**

We are attached to what we think will give us a sense of life. We have deep affection for the things that seem to make us feel better about ourselves. These attachments and affections are our externals.

To live the life you want to live, you must identify your externals. Until you eliminate the hold these have on you, you will be enslaved to them.

The world system wants men to be consumers, workers and orbiters to keep the machine rolling (without complaint). Men have been trained from the beginning of their lives that in order to get any of the scraps life has to offer they must put their heads down and accept an externally driven and defined life.

➔ **There is a different way to live.**

Reflection Questions

What do you think of first when you her the idea of the externally referenced life?

From the list, which externals seem to be strongest in your life?

How do you think these externals developed in your life?

In what ways has your life been lived out from an external authority?

Which parts of your life have been lived out from your own inner authority?

Where did you learn that you are broken or flawed?

Whose voice does your "inner critic" have?

What do you recognize that you may be enslaved to?

Solid Challenge #3: Ownership Statement

Ownership means that I take responsibility for pretty much everything in my life. It means I do not see myself as a victim.

The externally referenced life is a life where everything seems to be "done to" you. It is a life where you are powerless and you don't take blame for what happens. It's a feminine posture. Let's change to a masculine posture that does life.

From the beginning of the chapter, list the problems you've been struggling with.

Where have you placed your reference point in your life; is it my woman, my work, my kids, family of origin?

What are possible lies you believe about yourself; I am broken, weak, good for nothing, powerless?

What people or things have been orbiting around in your life; my woman and her approval, my workplace, expectations?

Write an "Ownership" statement written to whoever runs your life that says that you are the one to take blame and culpability for...

...every problem you listed

...every external that seems to run your life

...where you have chosen to orbit

...the lies you have chosen to believe about who you are and what the world is all about

...the things you have chosen to orbit and center your life around.

It will start something like this.

Dear Whoever Has Been Running My Life,

I want you to know it has been my responsibility that I have been struggling with...(list your troubles)

It has been my responsibility that I have chosen to...(list your decisions)

Write everything that comes to mind and push through any resistance you have...

Take every category of this chapter and own that it is your fault and your responsibility that things are like they are in your life, even if right now you don't believe it is your fault.

Now read it to your mentor or your group of men.

2 HOW DID THIS HAPPEN?

We live in an externally referenced world and men in particular have been trained to be externally referenced. Let's look at what keeps us locked into the matrix of the externally referenced life.

We have been fed different messages or ideas about life from many different places. Here are some messages from our surroundings which have influenced our frame of reference.

As you become more familiar to this concept of reference you will see many more places in life that has pushed you and other men into an external reference.

Systems

Whether you are aware of this or not, we are all part of various systems through which we live out our lives. These systems are significant contexts of our experience and gaining understanding will open your mind to clarity about how your life is externally referenced.

A system is a group of connected people that come together to make a complete whole for accomplishing some kind of purpose or even for survival. Families, a church, your culture or even your country are systems in which you live.

It is essential that you understand your role in any of these systems so that you can begin to make changes in your frame of reference.

Usually we accept these roles without any consideration or intention. We blindly begin to follow some unspoken expectation in order to keep the system rolling along.

When we break free from our expected role, we will rock the boat and the system will do all it can to put you back into the Status Quo. It is like your body system that does all it can to keep things at 98.6 degrees. The internal homeostatic mechanisms like sweating or shivering keep it the same.

> **Expect every system you're part of to do everything it can to put you back into your externally referenced role.**

In any system, there are many different roles that you could have. You could be the one who keeps it all together as the glue or the provider. You could be a scapegoat or black sheep that takes the blame and shame. You could be the helpless one who needs rescued. You could just be the cog in the wheel that keeps the machine rolling or a pawn that is just part of a bigger game.

Neo from the movie *The Matrix*, found himself to be a part of a much bigger story than he was aware. He actually was an unconscious member of a large system that used the power from his body to fuel the machine. Once he became awake to this, he then took on a new role with a different system. His new role with Morpheus and Trinity was a kind of savior that began to break the hold of the greater system for everyone.

The Message = You must keep the system rolling, how dare you change your life at the expense of everyone else?

School

Everyone who has gone to school has had their identity shaped by their academic experience. The fact is that the majority of us don't fit in the preferred learning style that is required to do exceptionally in school. Generally, about one quarter of us actually have the style of learning where school is just awesome! To varying degrees half of us end up doing alright, but it's still clumsy and takes work, but we get through it. Then the final one quarter of us are outright rejected and spit out into the cold world.

So for three quarter of students, school was probably not so positive. We were left with the belief that we are flawed and as kids, that hits us where it hurts – our worthiness. In addition to that, most of us were teased or bullied to some degree.

I was in the middle group, where I did well enough to get by in school. I am smart enough to do the work and get ok grades, but school still was a place of tons of shame. I would never ask questions, since that would point you out as being stupid or not knowing the answers. I was a big, chunky kid and had to deal with bullies. Teasing was a huge source of angst for me. School was tough for me, but not even as rough as some stories I've heard.

For most of us, we began to believe something was wrong with us. We had to figure out what we needed to do to fit in, to be acceptable and how we must be in order to keep the world rolling.

This is not the teachers fault – ok, maybe some teachers – but they are just part of a big system in which we all are expected to fit. But many of us don't fit and so we experience difficult things. Just ask people about their school experiences and you'll be shocked.

The Message = Something is wrong with you, you don't fit in. In order to fit in, you have to be a certain way.

Agriculture to Technology Shift

Over the last 150 years our world moved from a physically driven world of agriculture and industry to information/tech-driven world. This has created significant changes and expectations for all men.

We moved from work that required physical strength to work anyone can do. Consider what it took to drive a dump truck; years ago it took strong arms, a long reach and transmission mastery. Now even the most massive machines can be driven with ease, by just about anyone who wants to.

Since strength is a huge masculinity concept, men have lost a part of their core. Through technology, just about anyone can do just about anything, so many men question how we fit in the world. There are still trades and dangerous or dirty jobs reserved for men, but they are often seen as lower or less worthy.

My dad worked with his hands. He worked as a mechanic, on an orchard and as a millwright in a plywood plant. He could fix anything. And he did his share of creating machines to do specific jobs.

I remember him saying things like, "You can't work sitting down!" I know he was referring to taking too long of a break, but now as I sit counseling men, that statement seems to haunt me, questioning if my work is valuable. My dad is from a world gone by.

The story of Mr. Incredible from the movie "The Incredibles" illustrates this well. Mr. Incredible had been a super hero who saved lives and protected the world from evil. But the government shut that down because of liability. The movie begins with this strong man in a tight cubicle with his vitality draining every minute. His strength is no longer valued or even necessary.

This is the story of every man in this present culture. Our strength and presence is not as obviously valued as it was decades ago. Since strength is a significant part of the masculine core, and strength is not valued, we question our core.

The Message = With technology, Anyone can do anything, so your physical strength is not valuable.

Consumerism

Consumerism and marketing tells you that you're not complete without buying some thing. You only will be fulfilled if/when you get whatever it is that is being sold. You are told you need things outside of yourself in order to be whole. You need that new car or newest technology.

Look at how marketing has sucked you in. You need the newest gadget that you can't live without. You wish you had the nicest car to look cool. If you drink a certain beer women will flock all around you. All these things are presented to you as life-giving and essential to feeling good about yourself, to fit in or to compensate for all your inadequacies.

Consumerism came to the height of absurdity after 9-11. We heard that it was our role in this world is to keep the economy rolling, either through buying or working. In the middle of a major disaster we were encouraged to keep spending, don't let the terrorists win, and keep the economy rolling. This is who you have become; a consumer.

The Message = You are incomplete, so you must buy stuff or keep the machine rolling to have some value.

Pop Culture

Men today understand the value of manhood and masculinity from external resources. We learn our masculine identity from TV, Pop-culture, movies, news, women, men, and commercials. Every avenue of information hits us with information about the value of masculinity.

The models for masculinity we see are hyper-masculine like James Bond, Action Movie heroes, Sports figures, Dos Equis man, MMA fighters and the like. Or weak men like Homer Simpson, Ray Romano, TV show idiots who are absent, weak, deadbeats or SNAG's (Sensitive New-Age Guys).

It seems we are left with only two options – the hyper-masculine alpha male or the uber nice beta guy. Not much in between. Two significant parts of being a man - our masculine strength and our masculine heart are discredited.

I chose the nice-guy to be my way of life. It seemed to fit me like a glove. I knew I had a very sensitive heart, but I did not know what to do with my strength and desire to be stronger. I did not have much of a spine and did not stand up for much at all. This resulted in a deep, underlying anger that hung around in my life. Someone observed this as though I had lava just under the surface ready to blow. Only I did not let it blow, very often, because I was a nice guy. I did not know what to do with that anger.

Since masculinity is not generally valued and since we are inherently masculine at our core, we get a feeling that we are not valuable. Just so you know, the Solid Man Process has a third really good option.

The Message = Something is wrong with you, just for being male.

Religion

For an institution which would claim to set people free, religion has been is a major player in actually creating externally referenced people. The church has a mission, so you must do what is expected in order to fit in and so the church can meet its goals, even though those goals may be questionable.

It seems that morality and "right behavior" is maintained through guilt, shame and obedience. So individual freedom is lost. You must do what is expected and have the right lifestyle in order to fit in, to belong or to be acceptable. You must do certain things, adhere to certain beliefs and look a certain way in order to belong.

People are caught in the vise of "do versus be". Your acceptance is based on what you do rather than who you are. This has been going on for millennia; it was so much of what Jesus confronted with the religious order that was in power at during his time.

That religious order, the Pharisees, required everyone to adhere to a massive list of laws (do's and don'ts) in order to be acceptable. If you did not follow the rules you were shamed and rejected. Jesus challenged this way of living and faced significant consequences for speaking against them.

This religious way of life is still at play today in many houses of worship. Consider the way you may have experienced pressure to do certain things or perform in a certain way.

The Message = You must be or behave a certain way in order to fit in or be acceptable.

Family of Origin (FOO)

The family you grew up in has influenced you more than you will ever know. There are certain rules by which every family operates; don't tell the secrets, keep up the image, family first, Irish for life, don't give in, we stay together, us against the world, you will be successful, we all finish college, we are blue-collar, union for life, vote Republican, vote Democrat, or follow along to get along. Rules like this stay with us like barnacles. We must identify them in order to move into a new way of living.

There were also roles that you held to keep the family moving the way it was "supposed" to be. These roles look like; good boy, scapegoat, bad ass, smart one, hero, athlete, quiet one, or baby. You were trained to do what was expected and you certainly weren't supposed to go outside the lines! There are not many families who truly allow people to develop a truly autonomous self.

I took the role as the good kid. My older sister did her share of ruffling my parent's feathers and I was not going to disappoint them like that, no way. If I had any kind of need or emotional energy, I would just stuff it. Swallowing emotions was the job I did for my family, to keep it working. Later on, this fit perfectly with being a nice guy. I carried that role into my life and marriage, a perfect transition.

We all start out like the fish in water. A fish does not even know what water is. He was born into it and the water just always has been. This is like family. You may remember a time when you were over at a friend's house and noticed that Jimmy's family did things differently than yours.

33

That's the start of discovering the "water" you were born into. Later, you may have rejected your FOO or just escaped. Or you may have been locked in for way too long. Often we then will replicate our family system in our relationships, playing the same role and living under the same rules even though you are a man.

In this journey to be internally referenced, it is essential to consider your FOO. You may still be absorbed into the "blob" or realizing that you keep people at a distance just like your family. You must identify how the family trained you up and begin to break free.

The Message = In order to be loved and accepted you must follow the rules and play the role you were given.

Women and Relationships

While I believe that men and women are equal in the eyes of the universe, I believe there are significant differences. Our biology is quite different, our genetic imperatives are distinct, and the way we process life is unique. Respecting these differences is required as we process how we move in life. Most men have experienced some shame or even pain with how women understand men.

The issue here is not that women have an opinion about how men should behave, but that presently they have been able to determine what actually defines masculinity. So the message from the world of women is clear – "If you don't live up to our expectations about what we think a man should be, you will be unacceptable and we won't like you."

It seems that women actually "hold" the definition and value of masculinity. The ability to define another person and to determine a man's value, places women in an incredibly powerful position. If she is happy with you, then you are acceptable. If not, you are rejected. She has become your judge and holds your worth in her hands.

⟂ **Your measure is her pleasure.**

In our culture today it seems that women actually own the narrative of masculinity. It is because most men are externally referenced and have given away their power. Reclaiming our own power starts with being internally referenced; knowing who you really are and what masculinity actually is.

It is true that there are some wretched men and many women have experienced the evil presence of those men. However, the vast majority of men are very good at their core. The very small minority of bad men has helped create a distorted view of all men.

These good men need to stand up for the reality that masculinity is good and also stand up against the evil those men and women are capable of. Since women have had the power to define men, it is as though men need to have their manhood conferred onto them as though a woman would "knight" them with it. In order to feel whole or acceptable, an externally referenced man will need a woman to validate him.

There are other messages we have heard that speak to this – "Man-up", "You just don't get it" or "If women ran the world…" All these common statements show the common belief that compared to femininity, something is deeply wrong with masculinity.

The Message = You do not hold the definition of who you are. Therefore, to be acceptable you must meet expectations of women.

Designed for Connection

At first glance to some, the movement from externally referenced to internally referenced may seem increasingly selfish and creating separation or distance in a person's relationships. It may seem that this first pillar of the Solid Man Process is about creating selfish men who live in complete independence from others.

This process is counter-intuitive; it's actually the externally referenced life that's predominately selfish. It may seem to be other-centered and giving, but most of the actions of an externally referenced person ultimately are designed to bring something back to that person. In the externally referenced life, there are always strings attached to try to get someone to like them, to covertly get what they need or to be seen in a good light.

↪ **The externally referenced life is a life folded-in upon itself.**

The pleaser and orbiter may seem to be doing everything for others, even to the point of self-sacrifice, but their behavior always comes back to some if/then equation; "If she is happy then she will like me, give me sex, treat me right, or accept me." The focus always comes back to you in a warped, back-handed way. The pleaser is somewhat of a "mini-narcissist" because there are always strings attached.

The entire point of this first pillar is to help you become aware of your point of reference and shift it to a healthy pattern. The external reference is actually a very selfish posture.

Humans have been designed for relationship. There is no way to escape that truth. Our connections and attachments are one of the most significant and potentially fulfilling parts of life. It is that desire for close connections that makes the realm of relationship most frustrating as well. When they are not going well they can be one of the most painful experiences in life.

The internally referenced life will prepare you for deeper connections, closer relationships and more fulfilling interactions. When you are externally referenced, the world of everyone else is in your focus; what everybody else wants and needs.

You, yourself are actually not in the game. You do not bring "you" to the relationship. Not until "you" are actually in it will you ever have a healthy relationship.

➔ **Healthy relationships require at least two individuals.**

If you have given up your wants, needs and desire in order to please others, you are not an individual in the relationship and a healthy relationship is impossible. You must reclaim yourself through developing an internally referenced life. Then you can actually begin to experience deeper, more intimate relationships.

From the pleaser perspective, having wants seems like selfishness, but the freedom developed from the Solid Man Process results in deeper connections with yourself and with others. So let's keep the process going.

Reflection Questions

Of the messages you read which three meant the most to you?

What systems are you aware of that you are a part of? List at least 6.

What happened to you that your school experience moved you to be more externally referenced?

In what ways has the agriculture to technology change shaped how you see your role with work and career?

To what degree have you been affected by consumerism?

What Pop Culture images of masculinity have impacted you the most?

How have religious expectations or control played out in your life?

What were your FOO rules or your role in it? How are you still attached to those rules and roles?

How have messages from women impacted the way you live your life?

Which of the messages from the various systems have had the most significant impact on the development of your life?

Examples of Externally Referenced Men

Here is a partial list of examples of the shape that an externally referenced life might take. Read the list to see if there are any that seem to fit you, if so circle the number. If you wonder, ask your woman or your friends, they will have an opinion. Men who find themselves defined and driven by externals can possibly be described like this;

1. Raft on the Ocean; tossed about by the waves, wind and currents. They do not know what they want and are not intentional about where they are going. They are driven by wherever externals see fit to go.

2. Oblivious Marionette; where it seems like someone else is running the show and determining the next step. They defer unconsciously to what others want, controlled by external manipulation.

3. Passenger on the Bus; it seems someone else is driving their lives, navigating and determining where the bus goes. Externals determine the direction and path of their life.

4. Perpetual Adolescent; men who have never really been able to grasp or living out the fullness of masculinity, never really feeling like a man. In some ways like Peter Pan, living for the fun of the moment, bypassing the depth and responsibilities of life.

5. Sputnik; like a small satellite with no substance or gravity orbiting around a woman trying to please her. Like a planet, she ends up having immense gravity. This is very problematic for her because she does not want to be the strongest person in the room or the one with most gravity.

6. Nice Guy; men who live by the equation if I am nice or figure it out, everyone will like me and I will get the validation I need. They are covert with expressing needs or wants, not being honest, integrity in question.

7. Grass Eater; men who have completely embraced the "beta" posture, relinquishing or even rejecting anything resembling masculine strength and influence, except maybe within the gaming or technology world.

8. Sorry-man; men who are always apologizing for what they do, even to the point of apologizing for having wants. They don't want to be a burden on anyone, rarely ask for help and sometimes apologize for existing.

9. Mr. Fix-it; men who are always fixing everything; relationships, situations, conflict, if there is tension they fix it and do everything they can to reduce the tension or conflict. Others begin to feel like broken things to be fixed.

10. Tough-guy; men who have a hard, impervious shell never letting anyone know or see their true selves. They embrace a posture of walled up defense, not necessarily mean, these men are just unavailable and closed off to anything that requires openness and vulnerability.

11. Ass-hole-jerk; men who will hurt others with abuse, anger and meanness when someone gets too close. They embrace a posture of being on the offense, punishing those who expose their true, vulnerable selves.

12. Joker; men who deflect any tension or difficult emotion through humor. They are the class clown, having a face of humor even when things are

serious. They smile at times that seem creepy, because it doesn't fit the moment.

13. One-up Guy; this is the guy who always has a better story. He always seems to come up with an accomplishment or experience that is more dramatic or exciting. "Oh yeah, well listen to this…"

14. Blaming Victim; The Blamer rarely takes ownership of his actions. It is brutal for him to say the words, "I was wrong." He usually deflects accountability to someone else; finding fault in others or getting defensive.

Which of these examples fit you most accurately?

In what ways does it seem selfish to develop a more internally referenced life?

What questions do you have about how you must strengthen your individuality in order to deepen your relationships?

Solid Challenge #4: A Letter to Little You

This chapter is about the systems in which we find ourselves in life, Family of Origin, School, Work, Relationships with Women, Culture and Religion. Our interaction with these as we grew up has had a profound effect on how we move through life today.

This challenge will require to look back into your history and identify the most profound experiences you've had. Then you will have a talk with yourself about those experiences, through the form a letter to little you.

First, take some time to recall the most significant experiences you've had in each of these systems. Identify the age you were at that time, how that changed what you believed about yourself and how that may have changed how you moved in life.

It may be that when I was 7 my dad had to put my dog down. But no one said what happened to him and never talked about him again. My family held secrets like that. I thought I was crazy because I was the one who remembered. To avoid ridicule and shame, I made a commitment to never let anyone know what was going on inside of me.

Or when I was 9 I found a stash of porn in a shed by a field by our house. I thought the pictures were awesome, so I told my mom how cool it was. She was disgusted, told my dad and I got the worst spanking of my life. I learned something about how being aroused by a naked woman was dangerous as hell. Sexuality has always had danger attached to it. From that point on I hid everything about my sexuality. I committed to keep that area of my life to myself.

Now, write to your little self from your perspective as a man today. Consider how you would gently talk to your own son if he was going through this turmoil. Tell him the truth about what's really going on and about who he is. Let him know that what happened to him is not his fault.

Take at least the top three significant experiences in your life to write to your little self about. Tell the story of the event and write down the age you were when it happened. Then write down the commitments you made so you could remain safe.

Experience 1   My age at that time:

Commitment:

Experience 2   My age at that time:

Commitment:

Experience 3   My age at that time:

Commitment:

This will take some time. It can be a very powerful exercise. Take the time you need and allow yourself to feel deeply.

Dear_____(example; 7 year-old self)_____,

3 DEFINERS

Identity and Sense of Self

So far we have talked about the main shift that needs to happen in your life so you can actually begin to live your own life. An externally referenced man's life is driven, defined, soothed, directed and given meaning from external places and categories.

The outcomes of an externally referenced life are profound and sad. A man who lives an externally referenced life will never be able to experience the fullness of his masculinity and manhood.

> ☞ **The core shift to become an integrated man is moving from being externally referenced to being internally referenced.**

Your growth toward integrity requires that you remember and continue to intentionally engage in this lifetime journey. This process requires you to look deeply into the external patterns and paradigms you have had in your life, consider the shifts you need to make and then take action to change your internal realities.

The next couple chapters are designed to help you identify how externals define or drive your life. You will see how and to what degree you have been externally referenced in a number of categories.

You will find out which externals have had the strongest hold on your life and how they have defined you and driven your life.

Building Your Awareness; Externally Defined and Driven

To help find these internal resources, this exercise will expand on two main categories at the center of the external/internal shift; **definers and drivers**.

Definers are those things that define who we are (our identity) and also define what gives us value.

Drivers are those things that motivate us or give us impetus to move and do whatever it is that we do. Drivers are things that "drive our bus" and direct us with our next move in life.

This journey is about identifying external definers and drivers and then exchanging externals for internal definers and drivers; to become fully internally referenced.

This section has a number of categories which describe different ways you may be externally defined. As you read through the categories, some will resonate deeply with you and others not so much. Take time to see how each of these categories interacts with your life.

Definers; How is my <u>Identity</u> Externally Referenced?

Your identity is one of the most important parts of you; your person, your value, your worthiness, your personality, your character, even your story all rest within your identity. It is who you are. It is true that we are all like "snowflakes", unique with our own personal list of descriptors.

➔ **Your identity is who you really are.**

Let's dive into how your identity is externally referenced.

The following exercise outlines 8 categories which explain different ways we may be externally referenced with our identity. Pay attention to how each one makes sense to you as you read it. Many of these categories are similar and they flow together somewhat, that is ok.

Do your best to narrow down which are true for you. Have your workbook handy with the questions and write notes for each category. Have responses available for your discussion with your group of men.

1) External Point of Reference

An external point of reference is when a person's life is centered or revolves around something or someone outside of themselves.

Identifying at which point our identity revolves requires us to take a deep look at where we actually find our value or identity. As a kid we all were looking to our parents and people important to us to find out who we are.

This is a natural part of growing up for every human being. However, most of us were raised by parents trying to figure this identity stuff out for themselves. So, we were left with an externally referenced sense of self, where we are always looking to others for our value or worth.

Our parents, especially our father, were designed to confer onto us a strong sense of who we are. Since most dads don't do this especially well, we end up walking through life needing something outside of myself to make me feel better about myself – an external point of reference.

> ☞ **You have been designed to live from an internal point of reference from realities that exist deep within your being.**

I have already referred to Copernicus. He represents this concept well as he argued that the Earth orbits the Sun rather than the Sun around the Earth. The Sun is our point of reference in our solar system. For us, this is important, if our entire lives have been lived believing I need an external point of reference in order to be acceptable or worthy, we will fail to live the life we have been designed to live.

2) Reflected Sense of Self

A reflected sense of self is created when what you know about who you are is determined by what others think of you and the responses you receive.

Your sense of self is "reflected" off of other's opinions of who you are. It is like living in a Hall of Mirrors, where each mirror has a new look; fat here, squiggly there. You will never get a true idea of who you really are because every mirror is different and has a different look for you.

People with a reflected self do everything they can to fit in since they don't think who they really are will be accepted. They rely on information that people reflect back to them about how they are perceived. Their antennae are constantly on trying to detect any feedback that comes in facial expressions, tone or any other form.

> ➤ **A reflected sense of self exists when someone relies on others to determine their identity or value.**

With a reflected self, you always need to keep perceptions positive. So you always try to make people happy with you or prove that you have something to offer, or that you are likeable. You can never rest, since you are always trying to fit in. Our true identity is masked, because we don't know who we really are. We rely on others to determine and mirror to us our identity and value.

An example of the reflected sense of self is when we attach to sports teams. If they win, I win. My well-being rides with how the season goes. Observe how sports teams are marketed. The fan base is developed through allowing a personal and community connection, often creating a lifetime bond even if the team perpetually loses. This is brilliant marketing which uses a need to feel connected and belonging to something significant.

A solid sense of self is determined from internal factors which determine your value, competence and acceptance. Your worthiness exists from who you are and the internal truths inherently found within you; as a person, as a man and in the dignity found in every human being.

The value of your identity rests in intrinsic facts; you are unique, you have things to offer the world that only you can give, you have your own story and you have a good heart.

When you gain a solid sense of self, you no longer have to prove yourself or show others your value. You know that you are good enough and you are acceptable. Therefore shame has no hold on you. So, you can rest and your energy goes toward your passion and integrity.

3) Unsettled Questions

Unsettled questions are questions that haunt us and exist with us because our sense of identity is undone and undefined.

Discovering your true identity requires that you discover and settle the deep questions that you have about who you are. Often these questions exist because of wounds or false messages from childhood.

These haunting questions look like; "Am I good?", "Am I good enough?", "Do I have what it takes?", "Am I acceptable or lovable?" or "Am I capable?".

> ↪ **To try to answer our question we will seek externals like women's validation, winning at sports, success at work, looking good or any one of a million counterfeits.**

When any of these questions remain unanswered or unsettled, a man moves through his life feeling weak, impotent, like an impostor or poser. There is a sense of incongruence and lack of integrity; something's not right. With this unsettled identity, we keep the cycle going by trying to get externally referenced validation from our "drugs of choice"; porn, women, work, looking good, the list is endless.

A solid man knows who he is and who he was created to be. His identity is founded internally from true factors that exist within himself. His identity is not defined by external judgments, opinions or expectations.

For healthy development, boys need an external point of reference to develop their initial sense of identity. When done in a healthy fashion, this sense of self becomes solidified and as a young man he does not need external validation or external definers to tell him who he is. He knows that his heart is good and that he has what it takes to handle anything life brings. His questions are settled.

This is the job of the father; to communicate to the child that they are enough, that they have what it takes, that he likes them and that he knows that they will do just fine as they engage with the world.

The father's voice says, "I am proud of you." "I believe in you." "You are my beloved son and I am pleased with you." "You will do just fine." or "You're good at that." But for most of us, this has not been our experience with our dads.

Usually we've been given opposite messages and our questions remain unanswered because of our father's silence, disengagement or scorn. This has left us with a few generations of men with profound unresolved questions.

Your journey requires a sort of "re-fathering". You will need to do the job your father left undone. This will be you taking the time to attend to your own unsettled questions and resolve them yourself from a deep internal place.

⮕ **You may just have to re-father yourself.**

Since most of us have not received this blessing from our dads, the journey of a solid man will be spent taking the time to discover the truth about who he is; his design, his strengths, his weaknesses and what makes him come alive.

A solid man knows his true name; a name that only he has, his solid identity. However, for most men external voices (parents, coaches, teachers, bullies, peers, siblings, etc…) have attached false names or messages on them throughout their lives.

These are names like Stupid, Worthless, Never Amount to Anything, Good For Nothing, Lazy, Pussy, Weak or a myriad of others. You will go through the process of identifying these false names in Pillar Three. Then you can set them aside, embracing only your true and accurate name.

A solid man knows his questions and has a unwavering answers to them, they have been settled. A solid man has an accurate identity, an internal point of reference, and he knows who he truly is.

Settling the question that has been haunting you your entire life is an essential part of gaining an internally referenced life. In the following pillars we will take time to build this into your life.

4) External Validation

External validation exists when we need something outside of ourselves as an external stamp of approval showing we have value or worth.

Because we have a reflected sense of self or external point of reference, many of us have sold out to living for external validation in order to feel good about ourselves and to somehow get the message that we have value or worthiness.

To get external validation we need a woman to smile at us, to keep people happy with us and to keep conflict at a minimum. External validation becomes our drug of choice and like a junkie when we need our drug, we will do just about anything to get our next hit. So we smoke the "validation crack pipe" as often as we can.

📖 **Since we have a weak sense of identity, we will even sell our soul for just a taste of validation.**

The main way men pursue external validation is through women. We will seek a woman to confer our manhood upon us (Dalbey). We will try to capture the elusive "Woman with the Golden-Hair" in order to find a sense of being or wholeness (Bly). According to Sam Keen, men cannot find themselves without first separating from the world of "WOMAN". Since we need validation, the woman even becomes our "god" (Glover). Notice how you interact with women to get your validation fix.

We think the woman is our source of life. The endless and futile pursuit of a source of validation from a resource outside of us requires an unsustainable supply of energy. So much so that this pursuit wears us down and drains much of our energy and time. We lose our vitality and strength. We don't have much left in the tank for what matters most; close relationships, your purpose and even caring for yourself.

Pornography is a profound example of this. In porn, a woman will be postured in such a way to non-verbally communicate, "I want you" with the "come hither" look. Like the song of the siren, this works to draw any susceptible man into her web.

What is commonly called "Sex Addiction" is actually "validation" addiction. It is true that sex is the context of the struggle, but it is really all about the need to validate a weak sense of self. The good news is that as your sense of self becomes more internally validated, any "Sex Addiction" behaviors begin to fade away.

Another thing that happens with the need for external validation is that we put women in the position of "Judge" in our lives. We allow them to judge our behavior and our value. What they think of us becomes the supreme measure of whether you are good enough or not.

This is a huge reason so many men become pleasers and put their woman on a pedestal. Since she holds the gavel in her hand, we must do all we can do to make sure she is happy with us.

But now by taking this journey, you will begin to develop an internal sense of your value and the questions that have haunted you will become settled. You can begin to believe that you actually are good enough, you are acceptable and you have what it takes. Your relationship with your woman will have a chance to be built on a healthy dynamic.

More will be said about gaining a solid identity based upon internal realities, settling the questions and reclaiming the narrative of your life.

For now, observe in your life how you seek external validation and how externals impact your life.

> ➔ **An Internally Validated Identity is your goal.**

Gaining an internally validated identity is the antidote to sex addiction and porn compulsivity. Developing a stronger, internally validated self, resolves your "Validation Addiction". As you develop a stronger sense of self, the role of porn and sex will change dramatically in your life.

5) External Soothers

External soothers are various things in our life that we use to manage or reduce our anxiety and fear. We use external soothers to escape and numb difficult emotions or situations. We use them to keep us from being overwhelmed with real life.

For men who struggle with lack of integrity, how we sooth our own anxieties, fears and moods is a major factor. Soothing could be anything we do that would eliminate or diminish difficult emotions, anxiety, fear or some internal turmoil.

We may sooth ourselves through substance abuse, acting out sexually or even being passive. There are thousands of options for self-medicating our anxieties by using our personal "drug of choice". Somewhere in life, external soothers like substances, sex or validation have become tools to calm, numb or escape difficult experiences. To handle difficult experiences or emotions, numbing and escaping seem to be our only options.

The external mechanisms which function to soothe or eliminate anxiety, shame, depression and other difficult emotions always divert our eyes away from where the attention really needs to be; the heart. Our heart or soul needs attention but we get distracted with externals thinking that we are calming ourselves down, when we are just escaping important parts of life that need attention.

To care for our heart we must listen to what it is telling us and then do what our heart is guiding us to do. We must soothe ourselves from an internal place that is centered on our true identities and openness to our internal realities.

> ➔ **Listen to your heart; it has prime information to care for yourself.**

The solid option is to stay with the difficult emotions and anxiety with questions like, "What is going on inside me?", "What do I need right now?" or "What information is my anxiety telling me right now?" If you stay with the difficult feeling and lean into it, you will discover valuable information which will inform you about what you need to do in your life in the present moment.

This is very different than what you have heard about anxiety. Many professionals will just give you a pill (another external) and bypass your internal processes. Staying with the difficult experience or emotion, learning from it and moving through it, requires a strong development of internal soothing practices.

The most beneficial practice is just breathing some deep breaths. From there, maintaining consciousness and awareness of all your internal process and external surroundings is essential for developing informed movement. Looking to externals to soothe your pain is a tough habit to break, however, you can break the cycle.

6) Comparison, Conformity and Proving Yourself

These are categories which we need in order to put ourselves in a situation where you need to feel good enough or even better than others. It is using interactions with other people to try to find your value, worth or significance.

Comparison; Many of us fall into comparing ourselves with others to see if we are good enough or even the best. To feel good about ourselves we try to fit in, find our place of belonging or force our way through winning. Whether we are trying to keep up with the Joneses, be perfect, engage in the rat race or follow the winning sports team; we often get caught up in getting our worthiness from external comparison with others. This is commonly called one-up-man-ship, where we always are trying to get one step up above someone else through various means like sarcasm, competition or being a know-it-all.

Sometimes this is socially acceptable like getting good grades or winning at sports or unacceptable like put-downs or bullying. Comparison will rip the life right out of you; you will never be enough or have enough. The guy next to you will always have a bigger dick, more muscles, more money, a better looking woman, more hair or good looks. An internally referenced man is satisfied with what he has.

☞ **What you have is enough. Who you are is enough.**

Conformity keeps you from being true to yourself and living with integrity. You will always lose your true identity when you try to be like others in order to fit in or look acceptable. The conformist is unsure if he will be accepted or not so he tries to fit in so he will belong. He conforms to whatever the shape the group dynamic takes. If the group likes country music, so do I. Or whatever that group is into. Sometimes conformity looks like being "Cool". Looking cool has been a cultural phenomenon for decades. Everybody wants to be seen as cool. Cool is just another form of external reference based on conformity and comparison.

☞ **You must break free from the need to conform in order to reclaim a solid internal integrity.**

Proving Yourself; Many of us find ourselves proving ourselves over and over. This is an endless game because if your internal is not in order, you will never stop needing to prove your value or worthiness. We waste a ton of energy keeping our flimsy identity shored up by various actions and accomplishments.

It is important to set yourself free from the game of proving your value from things that are fleeting and actually do not represent your value as a person. If your identity, sense of value and desire to fit in and belong is based on externals your life will always be owned by those externals. You will forever need to do what is required by the crowd to fit in. You become a slave to the opinions of others.

7) Perfectionism, Getting it right and Figuring it out

These are categories which we embrace as tools that show that we have it all together; which expresses to the world around us that we are actually acceptable and good enough.

A man who is externally defined is continually using the vast majority of his personal energy and resources to show his value or to prove his worthiness to the world around him. He is committed to and even obsessed with making sure that the perception of others is positive. He lives to make sure he saves "Face" because his reputation is so important.

He must get it right and figure it out in order to come across as one who has it together or is competent. He lives to maintain a level of perfection to keep his personal acceptability intact.

This is why it is so rough when your woman says, "You just don't get it!" That statement causes an externally referenced man to go crazy trying to figure out what it is she's talking about. And that's the problem to begin with.

These endeavors are fool's gold, with no true value attached. Any person who has spent their lives pursuing perfection has discovered (or will soon discover) that perfection is impossible to obtain, let alone maintain.

Most who are shackled with perfectionism received this from parental expectations. It is time to see what perfectionism really is and unchain yourself from these childhood-formed commitments and expectations.

The gut-punch from not feeling acceptable is shame. If I cannot keep up the image of being acceptable you discover something is not right about me. That is shame. You have this deep sense that something is wrong with you. Deep inside you know you cannot keep up the image of perfection, so you beat the tar out of yourself for being flawed.

⮞ **Guilt says, "I made a mistake." Shame says, "I AM a mistake."**

Unshackling yourself from perfectionism and the shame which comes when you fail to be perfect or have inadequacies requires that you recognize the utter futility in trying to achieve perfection. You must uphold the necessity to accept yourself with all your foibles and shortcomings.

One core aspect of being human is our propensity to make mistakes and carry significant aspects of imperfection. So if you are trying to gain perfection by getting it right all the time not only are you rejecting what it means to be human, you are attempting the impossible task of being perfect or trying to be like God.

⮞ **Perfectionism will kill your soul.**

So, you must reject perfectionism in all its forms with strength and learn to accept and embrace who you really are with non-judgment and self-love. You must accept your imperfections and know that even with your inadequacies you carry strong and indestructible acceptance and value, internally.

Often the person stuck in perfectionism is unable to take accountability for their mistakes, since mistakes reveal inadequacies. They do their best to cover up or deflect blame. It would blow away their "house of cards" if the truth of their inadequacy came out. So they rarely say "I was wrong."

↪ **With an internal reference a man can walk in confidence even with his many inadequacies.**

8) The Mask or The Chameleon

Many men have developed a life of hiding behind a mask. A mask is designed to hide someone's true face while showing a façade that's different than reality. Often what we think about ourselves is unacceptable, so we fear that our inadequacies will be exposed. So we create a mask to fearfully hide our true selves. We think the mask will be acceptable.

The Wizard of Oz is a great example of this. When Dorothy and her three friends first met the wizard all they saw was a gigantic head surrounded by smoke and flames with an intimidating, booming voice. Then Toto pulled back the curtain to reveal the true wizard; just a regular old man frantically pulling levers.

The wizard was using a complex mask in order to make people believe he was great and powerful. Just like the Wizard of Oz, we'll do the anything to make ourselves look different than we really are; usually hiding inadequacies and trying to look cool.

↪ **Allow your curtain to be pulled back; it's the only way to freedom.**

The Chameleon is similar to the Mask in that the person is hiding their true self. This time it is using the fine art of being able to blend in. A real chameleon is able to change its color to fit in to any surrounding. When a person does this they do everything they can to fit in and belong.

The Chameleon will change their way of speaking, interacting, commitments or even their beliefs. They will lie to show they have had similar experiences. A chameleon's sense of self shifts so that people will feel like they have things in common which then creates a false sense of connection and attachment.

Consider how you may have been hiding your true self through wearing a mask or changing your color like a chameleon. This is a devious endeavor which will always backfire.

Relational difficulties begin when you develop deeper connections, since the deception will always be exposed and people find out who you really are. If this type of external reference is the way you roll, you have your own history of these relational problems. I'm sure you could tell some stories.

⤏ **People are left with questions and confusion after interacting with a chameleon.**

The Mask is experienced in many lives as a Family of Origin construct as well. Your entire family system may have been organized around the rule of keeping face or making sure no one ever knew the family secrets. The family reputation or image was of highest importance. You probably are aware of the percentage of energy and focus your family had in order to keep "the show" going.

When you live in such a family, you are in a significant bind; because you are human, you need to be free to be yourself, yet you cannot betray the family or you will be rejected. To varying degrees all families wear masks. Consider the family rules that you lived under during the formative years of your life. The Solid Man process is designed to help you break free from these external systems.

More recently people have been able to create online images. You are able to be more handsome, be thinner, have more hair, or be taller. You can portray yourself as more successful or less troubled. You can make yourself look like someone completely different from reality.

These online personas are just another mask behind which we can hide. No one really knows who you are.

Instead of hiding behind a mask, it is important to allow your True Self to be revealed. While this is a strong part of integrity, it is terrifying. All your fears of exposure will need to be challenged and faced. Like the Wizard of Oz, you will actually find out that your true self is acceptable and capable.

External Definers Recap

Remember, this is about learning to develop an internally referenced life. Your value, acceptance and sense of worthiness must come from a solid internal source within you, from who you are. You must identify how your identity has been defined by externals. You must refuse to be defined externally. You must discover your value, worthiness and identity from all the internal processes in you. You will find out who you really are and from there begin to move from that foundational truth.

While to a degree all these categories were in my life, my big definer were Reflected Sense of Self since I didn't even know who I was, Unsettled Questions because I was very unsure if I was acceptable or good enough and External Validation since I was always seeking others to tell me I was ok.

For most of my life my identity, value, and worth was entirely dependent on externals. I had a huge commitment to figure it out since I could not just be ok with mistakes or looking like I did not know what I was doing.

<u>Reflection Questions</u>
Which of these definers are most significant in your life?

If you were to place a pin on the spot in your life where your life revolves, where would it be?

Who are you usually trying to please or impress? Why?

What your reflected sense of self look like?

What are your unsettled questions?

Notice how you interact with women to get your validation fix. In what ways do you seek this out?

How have you given women the position of "Judge", where they can determine your value or lack of value?

How have you struggled with external soothers and using things to numb out or avoid difficult stuff? What have been your soothers of choice?
How have you relied on comparison, being cool, conformity or proving yourself to feel better about yourself?

Who taught you that you need to be perfect and how has perfectionism messed with your identity?

In what ways do you or your significant other struggle with saying "I was wrong"? What difference would it make in the relationship if this happened more often?

When have you worn a mask or live like a chameleon? What were you trying to hide?

How have you used an online persona to look better?

Solid Challenge #5: Who Are You? Finding Your Identity

Your identity is one of the most profound part of your internal resources. This chapter has talked about what has defined you in your life. As a man with an externally referenced identity you will always be on the lookout for the next thing that will help you feel better about yourself.

During the Solid Man process you will discover the truth about who you really are. Most of us are very externally referenced in our identity. We are defined by what we do and the roles we have. This only gives us a shallow view of who we truly are.

List the roles you have in life; Father, Husband, Coach, Teacher, etc.

When men meet each other we always ask, "So, what do you do?". We are defined by our jobs or what we have accomplished.

List what you do for work, or what you have done in your life.

We are so much more than what we do. Rather than organizing our identity around what we DO, it is important to allow ourselves to BE. We must begin to be who we are. So this challenge is the start to a process of self-discovery of your true identity.

When you lose track of time, what do you find yourself involved in?

What makes your heart come alive? Or impassioned?

What are some ways you go through life that is uniquely you?

Describe your character and who you are to the best of your ability.

What would others say about who you are? Ask some of the closest to you to answer that question.

Now compile a list of what you listed. Highlight the characteristics that seem to have the most meaning to you.

Think of three arenas of life where you can begin to test if your true self is acceptable. We usually think if people truly knew us, they would reject us. Test that to see if it true. Find out if you will be rejected. Push into your fear to find out the truth.

  1.

  2.

  3.

This is a strong start. Knowing who you are from your deep heart will be the most important part of this journey. We will do more work to develop a stronger identity in future pillars.

4 DRIVERS

Intention and Motivation

Men who have an externally referenced life have given up their motivation and intention to externals that exist in their lives. This is not a personal or intentional choice, but somehow over time, this style of living developed. This shift happens when we unintentionally begin to go along with the flow all around us. When we are driven by externals we cannot lead and we don't even have control over our own life.

Men living an externally referenced life have a pattern of "Damned if I Do, Damned if I Don't" (Diid-Diid) and eventually develop a "Don't" posture of passivity, silence and isolation. This is because they are trying to hit external targets like pleasing a woman or making her happy. Eventually we learn that while we hit the target sometimes, we usually miss since it is a moving target. So we develop Diid-Diid.

I remember when I first heard this concept. It fit me so perfectly. I totally felt like this and so I chose to be frozen and passive. I felt like I couldn't move or speak. This passivity really fired up my wife and so I was really in a mess since I was always trying to please her.

Diid-Diid is the essence of external living. If we live to please others we often miss the target and fail to "get it". Fortunately, there is a target you can actually hit every single time; your own internal target – that is, what you want or what you know is right. When you aim for your target, you'll start to "get it".

This sounds very selfish to most men; but to live in strength and freedom, you must live to please yourself first. You must live from internals. Exchanging externals for internals is <u>the</u> shift to move you toward integration and freedom. You'll never become a man of integrity if externals control or direct your life.

This chapter will show how you are driven by externals. When you begin to see how externally controlled you are, then you can take back the reins in your life.

Just like chapter three, go through each of the categories and the questions in your workbook. Let your men know what you have found about how externally referenced you are when it comes to your motivation and intention.

1) External Drivers

Drivers are those things that motivate or create action in our lives, things that push us to do what we do. Drivers can also be things to which we react or things from which we withdraw.

Every man has been designed to be driven from an internal place. This internal place has been called many things; your heart, your soul, your core, your gut. Whatever you call it, this internal thing has been designed to be the driver of our lives. I will use the words heart and core to describe the internal process which includes your mind, emotions, intuition, and spiritual aspects of who you are.

Our problem is that we have become separated from our internals and given in to externals to tell us where to go or what to do. We do this when we live to please our women or try to make them happy with us. We do this when we allow our workplace to dictate our schedule or how much energy to put into work. We do this when we feel like we have no say in planning holiday events with family. We do this when the expectations of others determine our next choice in life. You do this when externals drive your life and determine your next move.

> ❧ **It is time to drive your own life.**

Our emotions, spirit, wisdom and intuition are what guide us toward discovering what the heart needs.

Men traditionally have stuffed away their emotions for a number of reasons and in so doing have stuffed away their hearts.

It is time to cease being like a raft on the ocean, floating where the current, wind and waves take you. You must drive your own life by understanding and being connected with all of your internal processes. You must get your heart back. Your heart will guide you where you need to go at any given moment; in real time, planning and discovering your purpose for your life. We must become internally referenced men. We must take the wheel of our lives and drive where we want to go.

2) External Accomplishments

Accomplishments are those things we have achieved and finished in our lives. This could include degrees, awards, goals or winning.

Externally driven men seek acceptance by accomplishing certain things or making sure that they win or are right. Often, we must achieve certain things in order to be acceptable, so we become driven to accomplish things that will make us look good. It could be anything. I might need to get a muscular body, straight A's, a championship ring or partnership in the firm in order to be acceptable.

Externals drive the direction your life takes, your choices in life and what you do. We can be driven to accomplish from external pressure; peers, family rules, vicarious expectations from your parents, cultural pressure, religious pressure, work pressure, materialism, status, and many other forms.

Our personal energy is spent seeking an unattainable goal through accomplishment. That unattainable goal is increased personal value from external accomplishment. Not until we actually achieve the goal do we discover that it does not fill the emptiness we have. The championship trophy looks good and the accomplishment was great, but the excitement lasts a few weeks, and doesn't really fill the void.

⋑ **Accomplishments never increase personal value.**

If you've been driven to achieve an external validator, especially when you don't get the goal, you really feel the void or emptiness. Any accomplishment or external achievement will never fill the void of an externally referenced identity. To have a solid life, your life must be driven by internal realities.

In contrast to being driven by accomplishments or achievement is the concept of rest. Rest is the ability to just be; to be who you are without external pressure to do what everybody else expects.

⤳ **Don't waste energy proving yourself.**

Rest occurs when I don't have to work for my value or to develop worthiness, I can just be who I am and rest in the knowledge that I am good enough, lovable and complete in who I am. Therefore, I can be driven from an internal place.

3) External Moral Compass

A moral compass is a guidance system which shows you the wise or right way to move in life. It shows you where "True North" is in any situation in your life.

Your Internal Moral Compass develops from your value system. It is what you believe is right and wrong and what you have developed as a personal morality. We all have a value system. We cannot escape this fact no matter how politically correct or "no-labels" we try to be, we all place judgment on what is right/wrong or good/bad.

Consider how your values have been developed. Are they yours or someone else's? Has your moral compass been developed from internal or external categories?

Men who are reliant on validation and pleasing compromise their values and sell out to get others to like or approve them. A compass driven by externals will be determined by a woman's mood, what parents believe or expect, what fits in, the fad of the day, political correctness or whatever the crowd is doing.

This is where a man's integrated core will be lost, he will lose self-respect and no one else will respect him either. A man with integrity in most areas in his life might find himself lying to his wife to keep her calm. If he told the truth she might "go off" and be angry with him for a day or so. His compass or personal value is based on her reactivity and moods, so he tries to manage her moods.

In order to be solid, a man must be driven from two internal realities; 1) what he wants and 2) what he knows is right.

Developing an internal compass is about developing your values. It takes courage to develop a strong internal core of values and non-negotiables which drive your passion and purpose in life.

Observe and notice the values you have and if they are from external or internal realities. Take an honest look at your compass; you will be surprised how external it is.

> ➔ **Many men with a strong moral compass will lie to keep validation.**

Do you carry the values of your parents, your church, your political party or whatever helps you fit in? Many men develop a compass to belong or even to get laid (as in, "I will go to this church group, political rally, etc., because there is a cute girl") only years later to be entrenched in a system of belief that is not necessarily his own.

Clues that expose an externally referenced moral compass are criticism and judgmentalism. When we are overly concerned whether others fit into our mold of acceptable behavior, this is evidence that our sense of morality is centered at an external point.

Observe yourself and how often you are critical or make judgment of other's behavior. The judgment may not be just about morality (lying, sexual behavior, etc.), but also how someone does something like driving, clothes or home maintenance.

Consider how often you do this and how this reveals how your compass is externally referenced. An internally referenced moral compass doesn't often pass judgment because you know you are able to control only one person in this life – you. And you allow others to live in freedom to make their own mistakes and be responsible for their own actions.

As you start to develop your own internal compass, base it on what you see as good or right. You will use external standards (laws, Scripture, philosophy, etc.) to develop your personal compass. They will be accepted as your own as you develop your own internal worldview or belief system.

When you have a strong internal moral compass, you will be able to stand for what you know is right, even to the point of death. This sounds extreme, but that is what defines a solid internal compass. Your compass holds your personal, deeply held beliefs about truth, right and wrong, even about life and death.

4) External Locus of Control

A "Locus of Control" is a fancy way of saying where your control of things is located. The locus is the point at which your control is happening. If you have an External Locus of Control, you are very interested in controlling things outside of yourself and your sphere of influence.

The truth is that you can only control **one** thing in life; that is your Self. In order to gain a sense of strength and power, many men engage in the futility of controlling others and their surroundings. If they can control people, they will feel better or in charge. This way of life always becomes frustrating and gets out of control, because you **cannot** control many externals at all.

The controlling of people results in some very unhealthy relational patterns; pressuring, bullying, abuse, manipulation and frustration. Overt forms of external control are physical, verbal and emotional abuse. More subtle forms look like guilt trips, passive-aggression, shaming, and silent treatments.

External control looks like managing moods, lying to keep people happy, covertly trying to get people to do things for you or to like you, beating around the bush, evading conflict, and not being assertive. It also believes the equation that if you give yourself up for others they will automatically meet your needs (see Glover's "covert contracts").

➔ **You can only control one thing – your Self.**

When we have an external point of reference we want to control the people and situations around us. This becomes a way of life with significant negative consequences; we become angry, frustrated, and abusive. Our relationships suffer dramatically. Some say trying to control that which we cannot control is our greatest source of suffering.

Integrity and solidness requires an internal self-control. Therefore, use your voice to communicate needs and wants, and then collaborate with those around you. You are responsible for taking care of yourself.

Use your energy to control yourself. Become responsible for your own sense of well-being. Developing a solid internal self-control will result in experiencing more strength and power in your life and closer, more intimate relationships.

5) External Solutions

A solution is our way of solving a problem or fixing something. An external solution is something we use outside of ourselves to solve or resolve our problems.

Early in our lives, as we build our externally driven life, we create solutions that depend on externals to solve the problems we face in life. We will rely on others to make us feel better, we will do things in specific ways to fit in, we unconsciously place burdens on others, or we make commitments to make life work the way we think it should.

These solutions are often subtle and go unnoticed. As children we build life commitments that work to keep us safe or acceptable. It is the best we can do as a kid, but it doesn't work anymore as adults. Sure, I got Mommy to think I was cute when I deflected conflict with humor, but my wife or boss becomes infuriated. Or I don't speak up at work because if I spoke up as a kid I was shut down, but now I am stagnant in my job. These solutions no longer have any benefit.

> ↪ **An external solution is relying on something outside of you to be responsible for taking care of your problems, pain or obstacles in life.**

A person who relies on external solutions will develop a passive stance in life which results in victimhood, consumerism, passivity or procrastination. In essence, this is relying on everyone else to make life work. Everyone else is responsible.

You must become aware of how you have relied on external solutions in your life. Procrastination reveals an external driven solution, I am doing what others want so I don't have the same degree of motivation as when it is something I want.
Waiting for others to decide what to do next is another. When we expect others to come through for you without asking or collaborating with them is another form of external solution.

When others are more responsible for your well-being than you are we see things like setting up your dentist and doctor appointments, making sure you eat well or wearing appropriate clothes for events. Waiting for your boss to outline your workload or what to do next is external solutions as well. This is like the posture of a child, waiting for others to come through for you.

If you allow others to enable you to be lazy or under-functioning, then we allow others to be responsible for us, which is another significant clue. If you believe your home is your wife's "territory" and you are waiting for her orders in the home reveals this as well.

Identifying external solutions takes ongoing work and observation. Pay attention to how you roll in life. Do you rely on other's to get you motivated or moving in a certain direction? It may just be at times that you rely on externals, pay attention and observe your motivators.

Developing your own internal solutions requires taking personal responsibility, soothing yourself, having ownership, caring for yourself, using your voice, asking for help, making plans and taking responsible action.

It is true that other people are a huge part of an integrated person's life, but they cannot be our primary resource for self-care or to increase my sense of well-being. The shift from external to internal solutions requires taking personal responsibility and developing ownership in your life. You must begin to grab hold of your own internal motivation in order to solve your own problems and to create the life you want.

6) Counterfeits

A counterfeit is something that looks real, but is not the real thing. They look like "life", but actually leave us lifeless and empty. They're decoys of the real thing.

We pursue counterfeits hoping to experience something life-giving and enriching. They will often provide a quick-fix or thrill for a moment, but they eventually result in emptiness, shame, angst or another negative experience. We seek sex, substances, things, accomplishments, validation, anything that will give us a sense that life is good.

The equation is this, "If I only had _____ , then life would be good". But when you get "blank", it feels good for a moment, but always ends up empty, sometimes with despair or shame. Sometimes, if a counterfeits has been at work in your life for an extended time you will face dire consequences; loss of relationships, work or self-respect.

➔ **A counterfeit becomes your drug of choice.**

The counterfeit is masking itself as the real deal. The real thing is actually your Source. Your Source is the true place that life comes from, your true source of abundance. The Solid Man Process encourages each man to engage in the process of discovering your true Source of life. Something or someone is the Source of life.

> ➔ **In order to be a Solid Integrated Man, a man must find his true SOURCE, where life is really found.**

We all seek a source even if we are not aware, it is just what we do as humans. Often we think an external thing like a new car, sex, a relationship with a certain person, a new job, more money, a house, some exciting experience, a substance, validation, or accomplishments will give me life.

We pick just about any external to be our source. However, all these things are gifts from the true abundant Source but are never intended to be the Source. But often we get stuck thinking "small" and pursuing materialistic stuff thinking these things are actually where life comes from. When we begin thinking this small, the gifts then become counterfeits.

A huge part of our problem is that we have attached ourselves to so many externals that fail to give us a solid sense of life. We have tons of counterfeits or idols. Some of which could be as simple as having a woman validate me or notice me to pursuing something that would make me feel like life is worth living; getting that right job or promotion, a new car, my next drug fix, accomplishments, or winning.

Consider what counterfeits you have had that's taken you on bunny-trails looking for life, only to come up in emptiness or shame. These counterfeits are sometimes called attachments, idols or illusions. Part of finding the true source requires you to list your counterfeits. We will do that as part of Pillar Three.

This is a part of the journey many men refuse to take. Since life is much bigger than you, to become the man you've been designed to be, you must identify your external counterfeits and find your true Source of life. Then anchor internally to your true Source with a consistent daily practice (also in Pillar Three).

7) Externally Driven Pace

Pace is an important concept to understand when considering external and internal drivers. Pace means the speed of movement as you go through life. It is the speed at which somebody or something moves, especially when walking or running. Or it is the speed of events; the rate or speed at which things happen or develop.

Pace is the rate at which life happens and flows. Sometimes we will feel like we are in a dream where life is just flying by. Sometimes things slow way down to boredom. We all have a certain pace that feels comfortable to us. And we know what it is like to feel out of control and out of balance when the pace is off kilter.

Reclaiming our pace is essential to developing an internally referenced lifestyle. Knowing what type of pace is comfortable to you is important. On vacation you will see people by the pool just reading and you also see people constantly on excursions always on the move.

> ➔ **Everybody has their own personal pace that is comfortable to them.**

We may have a partner that has a different pace, which can and often create tension. We also may be in a work environment that may not fit our pace of life. The work culture may be wall-to-wall stress and productivity with long hours and challenge. Work may be a place where you "hurry up and wait" with nothing much to do for extended periods of time.

Consider the pace of your life. Do you think you have much influence over how fast or slow things are moving? Does it feel out of your control as though you can do nothing about it? These are clues for you that you are living with an externally driven pace of life.

You have much more control over your pace than you know. You can be very responsible to slow things down and create margin in your life. You can speed things up and engage in more challenge if that is what you wish.

Having an internally referenced sense of pace is possible. You have to identify what pace is comfortable for you and then begin to make changes accordingly. You can change your job to something less stressful or maybe more challenging.

On your next vacation slow things down or get out there and do more. Talk to your woman about how you would like the pace to be in your home; less activities for the kids, create more margin or add some more intentional activity. You can slow it way down or speed it way up, depending on your personal internal pace.

8) External Authority

Authority means to have power or control over something or someone. People in authority direct or lead others to do what it is that they want.

Men who are externally driven often submit themselves to external authority. This is very obvious when someone joins a cult or something extreme like that. The cult becomes the absolute authority in that person's life. What they do, where they go, how they dress is determined by the cult.

This is not so obvious and usually acceptable in other categories. The military is a good example of this. You join the military and for a season they will tell you what to do, where to go and what to wear. When it comes down to it your leaders have power over your decisions and actions.

This could also be in a church setting, not as controlling as a cult, but still requiring consistent behaviors, a way of living or adherence to certain doctrines. Some demand that you live according to the Bible, but only how they interpret it. Often people use the Bible to rein you in to keep from sinning. At that point they are trying to be an external authority.

   ⮨ **Some people describe this as feeling like a puppet.**

More subtly it could be how your marriage is organized around your wife's moods. If your role in the marriage is to keep her moods level and you do everything to keep her anxiety at bay, you have submitted to the authority of her moods. You then may lie at times, since if you tell the truth she will "go off". This is managing moods and losing your integrity.

True freedom requires that you live from a strong inner authority. That means that you trust that you have a good heart and move from how it guides you. Inner authority is the having the freedom to direct and move your life as you please, from your own internal resources.

External Drivers Recap

Remember, developing a solid sense of self from an internally referenced point is essential. Your motivation, drive, purpose and intention must come from a solid internal source within you.

You must identify how you've been driven like a raft on the ocean by externals, refuse to be driven externally and begin the process of discovering your wants, needs, passions and drive from all the internal processes within you.

The drivers that have big to me have been Drivers since I have always felt like a passenger on the bus of my own life, Locus of Control since I have always tried to keep everyone around me happy with me and External Authority since most of my life was submitting to the authority of my family, school and church. I always thought someone else had to be in control.

Use your workbook to take the list of ways that we allow ourselves to be externally driven and number them according to which one is most significant in your life.

Talk about these with your group of men. Take turns outlining which aspects of the externally referenced life has been your main ways in your life. Discuss the outcomes and pitfalls you have experienced when you are externally driven.

Part One Conclusion

In this ongoing journey it will be essential to continue to consider how you are externally referenced in order to develop your internally referenced life. Continue to challenge yourself to be less impacted by externals and then begin to grow in your ability to be defined and driven from your good internal resources.

The purpose of Part One has been to open up your eyes to the "Matrix" of externals that have kept you enslaved. Part Two will help you open up your eyes to the deep, strong and dynamic internal parts of you that are designed to guide you into a life of abundance and vitality. We will Awaken Your Internals!

Reflection Questions

Which of the drivers have been most significant in your life?

How have you struggled with being a raft on the ocean or passenger on the bus and what can you do to become more internally driven?

What are your most significant accomplishments, how have they been externally driven? How has that external pressure pushed you to need to accomplish or achieve?

Observe and notice the values you have and if they are from external or internal realities. In what ways is your Moral Compass external?

What can you do to develop a stronger internal compass? What are things you might even die for?

What has been your favorite thing in life to try to control?

What have been your main external solutions and how have you deferred this responsibility to others? How can you become responsible for your own sense of well-being?

How have you struggled with counterfeits and pursuing things outside of yourself to feel complete?

Consider the pace of your life. Do you think you have much influence over how fast or slow things are moving?

What could you do to gain more influence on your Pace?

Consider where and how you might have placed yourself under the authority of something external of you. Where/How did this happen?

Solid Challenge #6: Who's Driving the Bus? Finding your Internal Motivation

Chapter Four has been helping you identify the ways in which you have been externally driven. The journey of becoming a Solid Man starts with discovering your true identity and then learning how to live from an internal drive. Following your internal resources will drive you where you want to go in your life. Let's assess your internal drive.

What has the externally driven life looked like for you? Some say it is the raft on the ocean, someone else is driving the bus or like being a boy. How do you describe it?

What have been the negative consequences of this?

Most men are not entirely externally drive, often there are aspects of life which are very internally driven like work or sports. What spaces in your life have been internally driven?

Why do you think this is?

Internal drive is found from our identity (who we are), our integrity (what we know is right) and our desire (what we want). Which of these are strengths and which do you need work?

Name three areas of life that you would want to be more internally driven today. Write 1 intentional move you could do with each area.

1.

2.

3.

If you were to make three changes to become more driven to make that happen, what would they be?

Write a paragraph about how you are going to become more internally motivated.

Group Questions Part One: The Problem

(This set of questions is for each man to present to your whole group)

In what ways do you live from an external reference?

Which externals have been strongest in your life?

Who told you that you are broken or flawed? Where did you learn this?

What externals do you recognize that you may be enslaved to? What or who has had the ability to control you?

What culture or system has had the most power on your life? Which message has meant the most to you?

How do you think externals were developed in your life?

In what ways does it seem selfish to develop a more internally referenced life?

Share with the group your top three Definers.

What can you begin to do to become more internally defined?

Share with the group your top three Drivers.

What can you begin to do to become more internally driven?

Share any more insights you had with Part One; The Problem.

PART TWO; THE SOLUTION, AWAKENING THE INTERNAL

Who looks outside, dreams; who looks inside, awakes.

- Carl Jung

Part Two Introduction

The Solid Man Process is about mastering the art of being good at being a man. It is about becoming free. After reading Part One, you're more aware of how your life has been externally referenced. Now you'll learn more about how to begin to live and lead your own life from an internal point of reference.

While Part One was a gut check to assess your point of reference, Part Two will move you into new territory, crossing a threshold into a new place. This new place requires you to live from an entirely new posture. This new way of living will change everything in your life. Are you ready?

☞ **In order to be a solid, integrated, masculine man, you must have an internal point of reference.**

You learned that the problem is that you've built your life upon what others think, what others need, validation from others, what others expect and have deferred yourself to externals. You have handed over your power to externals. You have been living an Externally Referenced Life.

Hopefully the consequences of the externally referenced life and the problems that develop are now more obvious to you. Identifying how and why you orbit around externals is the first step toward regaining a strong sense of identity and intention in your life.

☞ **Rebuild your life with internal realities driving/defining you.**

It is time to learn how the unplugged life is lived and become reliant on your own internals. You will begin to build your own internal "Matrix" so you can live in freedom.

Part Two will identify and practice forgotten or neglected internal parts of your life. Listening to these internal resources will bring freedom, vigor and vitality to your life. This is a journey that takes intent, focus and patience.

The external reference has left the world with generations of men who are frozen, passive and silent. The strong presence of the good men in our world has been diminished.

This is what these pages are all about; many men have lost their good, strong presence in the world and I want to fix that.

The Solid Man Process is designed to equip men to engage the entire world with the powerful presence and strong voice that all men have. Men have been designed to be a **force for good**; to be an influence of safety and abundance in every corner of the world. As with many changes, this starts at home, in your little corner of the universe, with you.

➥ **Every man has been called out to be a Force for Good.**

Men are good and want to create goodness in the world. Most men have a deep desire to protect, provide, and to create environments of safety and health. A very small minority of evil men have painted a corrupt image of the design of the masculine soul.

It is true that there are men who are abusive and even evil. James Loder describes evil like this, "God created everything out of nothing, but evil seeks to return everything to nothing". People who destroy, abuse and control are evil. These people are not the majority and do not show the true design of manhood.

I have begun to think about how I will respond if there was a shooting or event like the Boston Marathon bombing. I am now more mentally prepared to stand in the gap if something happens because I want to be a force for protection and good in the world.

Listen to your own heart as you are reading these words. You know what you have been designed for. Your power and strength is for bringing good things to your world. Remember that you can change the world.

The Solid Man Process will give you the courage and strength to begin to break free from the silent and passive posture you've had. You will learn that your voice and your presence are two of the most powerful parts of your being. You will change everything as you begin to speak clearly while developing a very active presence in life.

5 SIX SOLID CONCEPTS

Mastery, Freedom, Integrity, Gratitude, Humility and Healthy Indifference are concepts at the center of the journey to become a Solid Man. It is essential to discuss them here to ensure that you know what these concepts mean and how they impact your life.

Mastery

A significant masculine concept is mastery. Men are designed to gain mastery over themselves and their world. Gaining mastery over your own life is essential if you are going to live the life you want.

> ↪ **Mastery is gaining expert skill, knowledge and outstanding ability.**

Mastering your life is about becoming proficient at being you and living out your masculinity with goodness, power, authenticity and intention. This requires instruction (often with a Master or group of men), a lifetime of practice and intentionally pushing toward new boundaries of excellence.

In life, we choose some things we try to master. Our work is often one of those things. Our world seems to have no need or patience for men who attempt to master anything outside of work. Even developing a mastery of work is not readily promoted. Furthering your skill base usually is driven by passion and purpose from an internal place.

The world is only interested in keeping the great machine going and you are part of that "assembly-line" world; "just put your head down, do your task and all will be good". Because of this, we've lost our heart and we've lost our spine. It is time to get your heart back, to master your life and be free.

To be the man you want to be you must develop mastery in areas of life that exhibit your passions and purpose in life. For this work, it is important to begin to gain the core skills required to master your own life. The first skill is to develop and internally referenced life.

Mastery of your life starts with knowing who you are and then gaining ability to move through life with confidence, self-control and intention. Mastery and Freedom are at the core of the internally referenced man.

To live life from the inside-out you must master your own internal resources, especially your masculinity. From there you will learn how to gain mastery and influence in your close, intimate relationships.

I have always felt like a "Jack of all trades, Master of none". I know this has been because of fear, fear that I could fail if I begin to become an "expert". Or that I would be ridiculed for trying to be good at something, when I just really am a fraud. This is just fear shutting me down.

Freedom

As a masculine virtue, freedom is essential in the life of every man. Most of us have lost our freedom. Freedom comes from living from the inside-out. Freedom is the ability to act freely, doing and living as you want, without undue restraints or restrictions.

> ➣ **Freedom is having the personal power to create the life you want, to lead your own life and to expand into multiple arenas of presence.**

Freedom is another very significant factor in masculinity. The desire and need for freedom is at the core of every man. For Americans, "resistance to tyranny" is actually in our cultural DNA, yet men find themselves in a position where they have submissively sold themselves out.

We've sold our soul only to obtain the dregs of external validation here and there from work or from women. Since we need something external to fulfill us, our "resistance gene" doesn't get the chance to rise up and fight for freedom. It is time to let that rascal out of its cage.

I think Paul from the Bible said it best, "It was for freedom that we've been set free; therefore keep standing firm and do not be subject again to a yoke of slavery."

It seems the Apostle Paul is saying that God actually wants us to be free. God is actually pleased to see his creation roam the land in freedom. Imagine that, God actually trusts that you will desire good things. He wants you to move with freedom and life.

He challenges us not to fall back into bondage. I believe the bondage he refers to is bondage to external "laws"; the external rules and expectations of religion and the "world". Our freedom rests on the foundation of an internal reference in life.

☞ **Externals enslave you, Internals set you free.**

This is probably the opposite of many messages you've gotten from a church or religious experience. These messages say that you need to live under the authority of the church, a set of rules or what certain people believe that the Bible says. It is as though living under a set of rules is where true freedom is found.

Contrary to that, true freedom is experienced as you live from your own inner authority and moving from the good heart that God gave you. Could it be that God enjoys watching you walk in freedom? Religious institutions have always had a set of rules; Jesus actually came to break those rules and to set us free!

To regain your freedom you must recognize how you rely on externals for your personal value and for permission to move. From there, you'll learn to move from your deep internal realities.

Pillar One is just the beginning of living life with an internal point of reference. It is up to you to take this information and begin to live freely.

Integrity

Men who struggle in life (in whatever form) have not developed a strong internally referenced core from which life is lived. The strong internal core is where integrity is developed in a man's life.

☞ **An externally referenced man has no integrity.**

In order to gain a solid life of integrity, the essential shift is moving from reliance on externals to living according to the guidance of internal resources. At the very center of this shift is developing internal integrity.

Usually the first word people use to describe integrity is honesty, or just always telling the truth. This is significant because honesty is a significant outcome of having integrity, but there is much more to integrity than being impeccable with your words.

Integrity is about gaining maturity and having an incorruptible solidness. Integrity is doing and saying the right thing, regardless of external pressure or whether someone is looking or not. Integrity comes from a solid core of character and internal strength. Integrity is a centered, grounded life. Integrity is Structure, Integration and Wholeness built into a man's frame.

➔ **Integrity is experienced only with an internally referenced life.**

Externally referenced men lose themselves as they do what everybody else expects and what would please others. They lose their soul and they lose their freedom. Since they work from outside resources, integrity does not exist. They've lost their identity and their core.

Their life is viewed through the lens of what others think and want. Since they have no center, they easily get caught up in porn, purposelessness, powerlessness, fear, anger, and anxiety. They have no internal frame or authority.

They get stuck and stagnant in life without any significant personal growth. If you've ever been stuck you know this is not good. Humans have been designed to continually move, change and grow. This work is about growing toward personal integrity and integration.

I know I have said this many times, but in order to build integrity into your life you must make the essential shift from being externally referenced to being internally referenced. From there you will begin to develop integrity.

➔ **Integrity will never happen if you are externally referenced.**

It is also important to understand integrity so you can develop it into your life. So let's look at the three aspects of integrity that define an integrated life; structure, integration and wholeness.

First, integrity in its essence has an internal ***structure***. A building with "structural integrity" will not collapse even under extreme conditions. The building has been built with everything it needs to maintain its frame. The structure is plumb, true and level. It is built on a strong foundation.

☞ **The designer made the building so it would stand firm and create a very safe environment for all.**

The same is true in the journey of a Solid Man; a solid, immovable internal structure is the goal. Structural integrity requires a solid personal core which comes from a deep and strong identity and an internally referenced life.

To develop structural integrity you will develop a strong frame that will not crumble under any circumstance and is safe for all who engage with you. When you have structural integrity, you will maintain your frame.

⌧ **Integrity is Frame; a solid structure that will not crumble.**

Second, integrity also is defined by ***integration***. Integration exists when a man lives in a full, holistic way, bringing **all** parts of himself into complete working order. Somewhere down the line men have gotten out of the practice of integrating important aspects into everyday life; therefore we have lost integrity.

Our culture has taught and trained us to disregard important parts of us so that we will continue to keep the machine working. We don't readily listen to emotional, intuitive, spiritual or even physical parts of our being.

In order to "get the job done" or to fit in, we've been told to suck it up and soldier on without attending to vital internal resources that exist within us. These internal resources have been designed to guide us toward a full vigorous life and we disregard them as though we've been hypnotized.

☞ **Integration happens when we bring <u>all</u> the internal and physical aspects of your life together into one "well-oiled" personal unit.**

Integration of all our internal resources is so important in this work. As you begin to notice how much you have disregarded your core to keep others happy, notice what begins to rise up in you.

Finally, integrity requires ***wholeness***, like an integer. Notice how the root of the word "integer" is the same as integrity. An integer is a "whole" number, not a fraction or only part of a number. A whole number is complete, lacking in nothing. A solid man of integrity is also whole and complete.

Being whole and complete means that you have everything within your being to live a life of fullness and vigor. Our problem is that we do not believe this truth. You must remember that you are whole; you do not need anything or anyone outside of you to complete you. You are a free standing unit.

- ☞ **The romantic ideal of "You complete me." is from the pit of rom-com hell.**

Depending on what tradition you come from, to varying degrees men believe they are incomplete or broken; that something is wrong with them or that they aren't good enough. We believe that we need something external to fulfill us or validate us. This is not true.

If you think you are broken and need fixed, you will look to someone else outside of you to validate you or make you feel better about yourself. This needy, incomplete posture is what develops into unhealthy, co-dependent relationships. Looking for someone to complete you is a recipe for relational disaster.

Carrying personal wholeness into a relationship is actually what makes it possible to engage in close personal relationships with intimacy. Becoming internally centered and validated creates the opportunity to develop healthy, inter-dependent relationships.

As you stand solidly on your own two feet without faltering, you do not need anyone else to hold you up. Saying you don't need someone does not make a very romantic movie, but contrary to popular opinion it is a foundation which makes for a healthy relationship. Your integrity is the rich soil where intimacy can now grow.

- ☞ **You have everything within you to live a life of fullness and abundance.**

Remember integrity is defined by three categories; Structure, Integration and Wholeness. When working through this exercise keep these ideas in mind. Your journey toward becoming a man of integrity requires that you develop a strong internally referenced frame.

The Solid Man journey is about becoming good at being a man. Becoming aware of the reference points in your life will give you the ability to engage more in presence and influence so you can direct your own life.

➔ **An order to be a solid, integrated man, you must have an internal point of reference.**

You must build an internally referenced life based on internal truths and resources found in your integrity. You must live from your solid core.

Integrity has always been something that has eluded me. I did great showing a mask of integrity, but I knew deep underneath there was incongruity. In my lack of self-acceptance I could not have either integration (because I did not trust my heart) or an internal frame.

Humility and Gratitude

The categories of humility and gratitude are essential as we move toward mastery, freedom and integrity. As a man becomes strong and internally referenced, the true test of his character will come in the form of humility and gratitude. If these characteristics develop in true form, then this process is working perfectly.

➔ **Humility and Gratitude are true results of an internal reference.**

Arrogance, self-righteousness and boasting are attitudes of the externally referenced individual. These characteristics show that a man still remains beholden to the external world. Again, this feels counter-intuitive since you might have been taught that an internal reference would result in grandstanding, but the opposite is true.

➔ **Humility is just speaking the truth about who you really are.**

Humility has no desire to puff up. Boasting is the energy of an external reference. Humility is content with what is. If I am intelligent or athletic, so be it; I don't have to prove it to anyone. Humility has no need to be better or less than others.

➔ **Humility is not thinking less of yourself, it is thinking of yourself, less. – C.S. Lewis**

Humility is developed as a man accepts the fact that the fullness of his being; who he is, his capabilities and even his acceptability do not come from his effort, they are gifts. The Solid Man recognizes that he is part of a larger story; these great tools for living well have been given to him for the betterment of himself and all others in his sphere of influence.

Humility therefore begets gratitude or thanksgiving. Since the goodness and fullness of life come from a source into which I was born, I only have one true option, gratitude. Thanks for all that has been given to me and bestowed upon me. Nothing I have has started from me; I am living with the goods that have been given to me.

A posture of gratitude naturally develops from the internally referenced life. Enjoy the experience of knowing you are not the pinnacle of the world and regularly say "thanks" for all that has been given to you.

Gratitude is actually a type of "superpower". It is a characteristic that lifts a person into a different kind of category in the world of human interaction. We often don't see enough gratitude in our interactions, it really makes a difference.

Develop a "Gratitude Practice" where you take time to say the words "Thank You" at least ten times during your day to people around you. Find ways to express thanks to who or what you recognize as the Source of Life.

> ☞ **If the only prayer you ever prayed was "thank you", it would suffice.   -Meister Eckhart**

Use your voice to appreciate people with appreciative words more often. Go out of your way to write notes telling people how you appreciate them. Thank people for normal things they do to serve you or for kindness. See what happens. You will be surprised.

I always had a phony humility that was based in shame and so I never really had gratitude either since I really was not thankful for my life or who I was.

Healthy Indifference

This concept comes from Bradley Fenton's book, _Stumbling Naked in the Dark; Overcoming Mistakes Men Make With Women_. He introduces the concept of "Indifference" as the illusive thing that attracts women to men.

Indifference is a characteristic in which a man does not care what a woman is thinking about him or about what the outcome of any interaction with her would be. The internal confidence he has in his identity is not determined by her.

Fenton identifies that as indifference is highly attractive to a woman, most women do not have the skill to discern whether the indifference is healthy or unhealthy. This is where many women get caught into the cycle of getting stuck with jerks.

➔ **Indifference is attractive to a woman, Healthy Indifference is a treasure.**

A jerk does have indifference; he does not care what a woman thinks or whether she likes him or not. Where it goes awry is that the jerk actually does not care about her safety or well-being. He really is an uncaring jerk. Initially it is very hard for a woman to distinguish between healthy and unhealthy indifference.

A man with healthy indifference is truly indifferent to whether she likes him or not, indifferent to her moods, indifferent to if she agrees with him or not, indifferent to what the outcome of any interaction would be AND actually is concerned with listening to her opinions, increasing her safety and increasing her sense of well-being.

While indifference is highly attractive to women, only healthy indifference creates a foundation upon which a good long-term relationship can thrive.

Healthy indifference is impossible to achieve while living an externally referenced life. The journey you are on first must be concerned with just plain indifference. You have to develop an internal referenced identity that is secure and solid.

You will need to gain a posture that essentially does not care about whether she likes you or which mood she has. You will need to get to a place that is not deflated or devastated if she doesn't agree with you, does not want to have sex with you or whatever outcome is important to you.

Once you have indifference, then you will be able to develop healthy indifference. You care about yourself and responsible for your well-being, now from that platform you can care for her safety and well-being as well. That is healthy indifference.

I could never have indifference, I was always so concerned about what everyone else was thinking about me. I was so concerned with what the possible outcomes could be, being embarrassed, ridiculed or seen as deficient. I was so worried, so I could not be free.

Reflection Questions

In what ways have you been frozen or silent in life? By what?

What might the world look like if every good man stood strong in his own corner against evil and was a force for good?

Since mastery is gaining expert skill, knowledge or outstanding ability, what might be the best way for you to master your own life?

In what ways do you feel free, stuck or enslaved in your life?

What needs to shift in your life to begin experiencing more freedom?

Of the three aspects of Integrity; Structure, Integration and Wholeness, which is the most important for you to focus on? Why?

In what ways have you developed "Frame" in your life? Or not?

What could you do to develop more integrity?

In what ways has humility developed in your life? How could you embrace this process?

What could you begin doing to develop a practice of gratitude?

What has been going on in your life that's kept you from having indifference?

What kind of responses have you gotten from people when you've had healthy indifference?

Solid Challenge #7: Checking In

Checking in is commonly also called mindfulness or self-awareness. Whatever you call it, it is a central practice of a Solid Man. To develop the internally referenced life, you must be able to check-in with yourself, often.

The personal Check-In is a practice that you will do several times a day. Pick times during the day when you will "check-in". This will be an opportunity for you to stop for a few minutes and ask yourself how you are doing, what are you feeling or experiencing and what you want to intentionally accomplish today.

Check-In happens when you take a moment to breathe and relax (you can do this at any time), then listen to your own heart. As you breathe, check in and pay attention to your thoughts, feelings, wants, solidness, connection with your source, intentions and whatever else comes to you.

Ask yourself, "Right now I am feeling_____." or an intention like "I want to be successful with my solidness today." Just talk to yourself about what you are experiencing; good or bad, difficult or happy, whatever it is.

Be open and aware of what is going on inside of you. Now take what you have identified that you are feeling, experiencing, wanting and communicate that to your Source of life.

Start with at least twice a day, but multiple times is best. Do a check-in when you feel difficult emotions, when you feel pulled to act out with counterfeits or whenever you have a free moment. Make yourself a reminder to check in often.

When would be your best times for you to check-in?

You can actually do a check-in right in the middle of moments of anxiety and tension (this is really a perfect time for check-in). In real time take a moment to breathe. Take three or even four nice, slow deep breaths.

Don't worry about what people think, just hold that space for a moment. As you breathe ask yourself how you're feeling and what you notice is going on. Ask yourself these questions; *What am I feeling right now? What is going on? What is my body telling me? What thoughts have my attention? What do I want right now? How Solid do I feel right now? How connected to my Source am I? What do I want to accomplish today? What is important to me right now?*

Don't be shy about talking to yourself!

6 TRUSTING YOURSELF

Your Internal Resources

Internal resources are where we get the vital information that helps us decide what to do, what to say or what action to take in real time.

In order to live a free, wholehearted life a man must reclaim the ability to observe, notice and discern his internal process and allow that internally gathered information to guide his life in the present moment.

> ↩ **A solid, integrated man is connected to his own internal matrix, then he can fully detach from the external matrix.**

The internal resources are the tools you need to lead your own life where you want it to go. To live freely, you must master listening to your own personal internal matrix instead of being led by what everyone else wants or expects from you.

There is so much more going on inside of you than you have ever imagined. The internally referenced man does not disregard his internal processes. The internal tools guide a man through any present event. When you master listening to your internals, you'll become confident you can handle just about anything in life, in real time.

> ↩ **Your internal resources are a goldmine of solid information.**

You'll need to relearn what you've been taught about yourself. For example, men have been led not to respect the emotional or intuitive because of ideas that it is illogical or feminine.

We all have separated from our internals to varying degrees. Integration of internals increases the richness of experiences and prepares you to fully engage in life.

In this second section, Awakening Your Internals, we've outlined what it will take to trust your internals, how to identify and disempower a great obstacle that exists in all of us, and then outline the significant internal resources you have at your disposal to live a life of integrity and freedom.

➔ **First you must learn to trust your self.**

In order to move into mastery and freedom in your own life you must trust your self. You must break out of your previous pattern of only trusting what others think and trust that your own internal resources will guide you well.

In order to live fully human lives, we must begin to learn how to intentionally connect and respect our internals. The journey of following your heart and trusting your self requires that you remain conscious, to know you are in good working order and to know the quality of masculinity.

Consciousness

Trusting yourself requires consciousness. Consciousness is being awake, aware and seeing what is going on. Do I know who I am, where I am, what time it is, what is happening? Am I asleep in my own life, oblivious to what is going on or how I could influence my world?

In his book *It's Your Call*, Gary Barkalow talks about being "alert and oriented x 4 (AOx4)". After a traumatic event, first responders ask if the patient can correctly identify the time, their name, their location, and the event. If they are conscious, they can answer all four questions, they are alert and oriented times four.

Many of us go through life unconscious; we are not present, we really don't know who we are, we are oblivious to our context and confused about what is happening around us. We must become AOx4!

Here are four postures to consider so we can wake up and become more conscious.

Become a Student

The **first** posture of consciousness is that you must become a "Student" of your self. This requires that you humbly realize that you have been oblivious to inner workings, forgotten who you really are and have lost the art of being fully human.

It is essential that you become a student, of yourself. The posture of being a student is the beginning and the process of the journey of mastery. The goal will be to master the art of being a man, being human and being you. So this requires the humility of embracing the fact that "I am not so good at this, yet". Being a student is the posture of any true master.

> **Become a student of your self.**

You cannot assume you know anything, since you've just gone along with externals up to this point. You've got to re-learn what you think you know. Take the humble posture of learning and you will do just fine. Learn how to listen and learn from your internals.

The posture of a learner puts you in a position where you don't have to have it all together. You are a learner because you don't know it all. This humble attitude releases the expectation to be perfect or to get it right. A student can engage in experiments that may or may not be successful. Success is the fact that you are free to explore and experiment gathering information as you go along.

Become an Observer

The **second** posture of consciousness is to become an "Observer" of your self. Observing means to actually watch yourself in action, to see what you do, to notice what you feel and experience, to pay attention to what moves you and interests you. Observing requires consciousness and being awake. Most of us just go through life in a fog just as the 'matrix' wants.

Observing is checking in with yourself; asking yourself simple questions like, "What is going on?", "What is happening right now?" or "What do I need right now?" To do this well, you don't have to accomplish anything, just to observe what is going on inside you. Just be aware, notice and continue to maintain consciousness.

> **Become an observer of your self.**

We are very critical of ourselves. So observing requires that we are non-judgmental. Dr. Robert Glover talks about becoming a "Non-Judgmental Observer of Yourself". We are our own worst critic; old narratives, our false self, the crazy voice in our head all come up when we feel inadequate, fearful or out of control.

Your internals are not here to be fixed, but to be listened to. Judgement, shame and self-attack can never lead to a good ending. Listening is a lost art. There is not enough thoughtful listening. Listen deeply to yourself without judgment and with curiosity. Soon you'll know just what to listen for.

The posture of observer requires that you put away the negative, judgmental critic. The critic has haunted you for too long, so in order to non-judgmentally observe yourself, you must silence the critic. Remember that nothing is wrong with you and just observe, gaining vital information about what to do next.

Become Connected

The **third** posture of consciousness is being "Connected" with your self. Externally referenced men live compartmental, disconnected lives. We use self-medication, like drugs or alcohol to escape or numb our emotional energy. We have disregarded our core experiences to get through the menial parts of life.

We have lived vicariously through others, like sports teams or your kids to feel valuable. We have lived to please others to keep them happy with us, all along missing out on our own needs and wants, dismissing them as selfish.

> ➔ **We are self-disconnected when we rely on externals for accomplishment or validation.**

To live a life of strong mastery, disregarding your self must end. Connect with your internal resources for your sense of value and worthiness. Stop living a disconnected, dichotomized and dualistic life. You must become who you really are, not some chameleon trying to fit in or please.

> ➔ **Be connected to your self.**

Connect with yourself. Start the process of finding out who you really are. Consider what you want. Dig deep to find out what you really believe about life and what makes you thrive.

Think about what makes you tick and what brings you passion. Take time to dream. Ask yourself what makes your heart come alive. Develop self-confidence through connecting with yourself and trusting that you have the internal tools to lead your own life. This is another way to become integrated.

Stay Present

The **fourth** posture of consciousness is staying "Present". Presence is about staying aware in the present moment. Presence means to stay awake and conscious and observe whatever is going on in you and around you. Presence requires that you stay in the present moment.

> **Be present with your self.**

What happens to us is that worry and anxiety about the future or regret and shame from the past squeeze out the present moment in real time. Both the past and the future press in from both sides like a vise, eliminating the fullness of what is happening right now, squeezing out the present. We end up living more in the past or in the future, but not in the present now.

> **Past Regret and Future Worry CRUSH the Present like a VISE.**

Becoming internally referenced and living from your internal resources requires that you live in the present moment. All the tools and resources you have can only be discerned and understood from what is happening at the present moment.

> **To live fully from the inside-out you must live in the "Now".**

You are in Good Working Order

Trusting yourself requires that you actually trust your self. We've talked about the strong message in our culture today that says you are broken, flawed or that something is just not ok with you. This idea comes from most religious, philosophical and psychological traditions.

As you read the heading, -You are in Good Working Order-, how did you react to the idea that "Nothing is wrong with you."? This belief, that we are flawed, is deep within most of us and it will be a challenge to break.

This idea is a big issue for almost every human. For now, just let the idea that you are not broken marinate a while. When you believe the message that something is wrong with you, you will never be able to trust yourself. You must know that you are good enough.

☞ **To move in freedom, you must trust your SELF**

We all have our own list of reasons why we have believed we are shameful, incomplete or flawed. Some of us have shame or feel that something is wrong with our sexuality, that you are a pervert, have a one-track-mind or labeled as a sex addict. Or that you're not smart enough, good-looking enough or skilled enough.

Your shame may be your incompetence, inability to remember, have follow-through or to be reliable. It might have been that you think you are not good enough, or have failed to achieve or accomplish and not measure up. Whatever it may be, if you are going to master living from the inside-out you must believe this;

☞ **There is nothing wrong with you, you're in good working order.**

If you cannot grasp the idea that you are in good working order, you will have a tough time moving forward. Developing your internally referenced life requires that you deeply trust yourself and your internal processes.

If you believe that your internal processes are flawed, you will not be able to trust them and therefore you will continue in your slavery to externals.

I am not saying we are perfect. I am saying we are in good working order. We make mistakes all the time. We continually choose foolish ways of living or we forget who we are and fall back into fear and self-protective defense. We "sin" all the time by choosing to follow various idols, counterfeits or attachments rather than our one true Source.

☞ **Your mistakes and "sins" are not evidence that you are flawed.**

What is "wrong" with us is that we forget who we really are and we fail to listen to our internal processes. When we allow ourselves to be defined and driven from externals, that's when our problems arise.

☞ **We are always trying to fix what actually doesn't need fixing.**

Many of us experienced abuse in our lives. Usually this results in a tainted view of our value. If someone treated you like garbage, then you must be garbage. You must process the ambivalence associated with abuse and know that it was not your fault or because of any flaw within you. It was that someone in your life abused you, not because you're flawed or responsible.

> ➔ **What needs to be fixed is your belief that you need to be fixed.**

Some men struggle with physical or mental issues like Low-T, ADHD or even bipolar disorder. Just because something may be imbalanced chemically or hormonally does not mean their hearts are flawed and their ability to feel, want and choose is broken.

You may live in the shame of significant mistakes. We let the mistake define us and so it sticks with us like a label defining our value.

All of us have some type of physical or mental imperfection. Some of us believe that since there is some problem, then we really cannot trust our internal processes. That is not true.

> ➔ **Don't live as a victim to your imperfections.**

Be responsible to take care of whatever the problem is, care for yourself and get as strong as you can. But remember that your heart is good and you can rely on your internal processes to be working just fine.

Let your imagination go for a moment; what would happen if everyone on the planet lived from their heart? Would it be chaos, war and Armageddon? Would it be peace, love and service? Where your imagination went reveals what you believe about people and the state of your own heart.

Another way to look at this is that you are a Ferrari not a Yugo. Most of us see ourselves as the human equivalent of the Yugo, internally flawed with no hope of getting better.

Remember the Yugo from the mid-eighties? It was one of the most epic automotive fails ever. They were cheap and sold like crazy the first year they came to the US. They won awards and it looked like a great deal. But then the cars started to break down, often. But worse than that was the complete lack of automotive support and parts to get them fixed. So they were junked.

We think of ourselves like that, something is inherently wrong with us. Since we've have been told this in so many ways during our lives, we believe we are an epic fail like the Yugo.

On the contrary; you are actually the equivalent of a Ferrari. It may be hard to believe that you are a fine tuned machine designed with more than enough power to move through your world in strong, influential and good fashion.

➔ **Not only are you good enough, you are more than enough.**

Chances are no one has ever told you anything like this. The messages have been clear that you are like a Yugo, but no one has ever told you that you are a thoroughbred. You are complete and have all it takes to go through life well.

➔ **To master your life, you must believe you have what it takes.**

To truly believe that you are complete and good enough requires breaking down a lifetime of false messages you've received. Be patient with this personal and spiritual process, it takes time.

To be clear, I am not saying we don't make mistakes or that we don't sin. Actually, I would say we make more mistakes and sin more than we know, especially when the Shadow Self runs the show. It is not because we are flawed or broken. It is because of beliefs where we think life comes from and subsequent foolish choices.

With an internally referenced self, you can actually take ownership and own up to your mistakes. You don't have to cover up your mistakes and hide in shame and isolation. You will be able to actually live in humble authenticity.

With a strong and humble posture of learning from your mistakes, you can take your mistakes as feedback or information to live internally and thrive.

Think of any failure not as failure, but as valuable feedback to learn from mistakes and move powerfully toward wisdom.

➔ **You are acceptable with no need for any modification.**

Don't forget your true identity and where life comes from. Remember you are good enough. Remember that life does not work well when you live from fear or pursue counterfeits (aka "drugs of choice"). Remember that when you forget, problems happen.

Throughout your entire life continue to master the fine art of living and leading your own life. You have what it takes to become quite proficient at learning how to live your life with strength and freedom.

Masculinity Is Good

In order to trust yourself you must know that masculinity is good. What does it feel like to read that "masculinity is good"? For the past 40-50 years men have been taught that masculinity is inherently flawed. Many messages say that something about being a man is shameful or the way a man moves through life is not safe or good. You may have heard about what it would look like if women ran the world or that every man needs a woman to keep his wild masculinity in check.

Somewhere we've learned that we need something to restrain us from harming people or causing damage. It is as though we believe that if we were truly free, we'd go on a rape binge or become an uncontrollable dick. This is actually ridiculous, because when you are free, great things happen.

➔ **Masculinity must be released, not restrained.**

Ultimately, in the American culture, if you have a penis you've questioned your worth and value in some way or another; believing that there is something wrong with being a man.

It is true that masculinity often is expressed and manifested in ways that may make some uncomfortable. Since masculine movements like anger, aggressiveness, large posture, physical strength, strong non-verbal communication and withdrawing from relationships often creates discomfort. It doesn't mean masculinity is bad or flawed. It just means sometimes a masculine posture is uncomfortable for some.

In our present American culture the feminine has been upheld as the human ideal; therefore since the masculine moves differently than the feminine, there must be something wrong with the masculine.

➔ **You cannot go to war against yourself and expect victory.**

This is the concept of false narrative on a grand scale. It seems the entire concept of masculinity is suspect and under scrutiny. Something external of the masculine has arrogantly deemed itself worthy of judging the value of masculinity; and it seems, to external sources, that the masculine has been found wanting.

If men allow their identity and value to be determined by an external, they will always fall short of whatever expectation that exists. Therefore, masculinity will never be respected, valued or lived out unapologetically. The value and definition of masculinity must be determined from within, from an internal place.

> **The value of masculinity is determined by masculinity.**

We must reject the image of the masculine buffoon from commercials and sitcoms. We must reject the swinging pendulum which has only two stereotypes of the masculine; the sensitive new-age nice guy and the hyper-masculine jerk.

We must embrace the truth that masculinity is best lived out with a strong balance of heart and spine, alpha and beta.

Know, understand and believe that masculinity is good and necessary for healthy community and family. Embrace the fact that femininity and masculinity are different and complementary, creating amazing relationship possibilities.

When either masculinity or femininity unconsciously moves from the Shadow Self (more on this soon) many negative consequences occur. These consequences don't define the value of masculine or feminine, it just shows that we move foolishly at times.

Your masculinity is a significant internal resource which guides you into life with vigor and vitality. Because masculinity has not been respected, we are hesitant to embrace living fully in our masculine. When this happens we miss our deep core and lose the essence of our manhood.

Masculinity is designed to be lived out with strength, courage, love and freedom. Masculinity has a core of integrity, passion, power for others, moving expansively into our world. Masculinity is good and developing mastery with your masculinity is essential.

For the longest time I could do none of this. I could not trust myself at all. I wasn't conscious, I was not observing myself, I was not present. I was very disconnected with myself and since I believed something was inherently wrong with me, There was no way I could trust myself. And I really struggled with what it meant to be a man. My masculinity was a place of confusion.

Chapter Six Review

Mastering the art of living your life in fullness and integration requires that you must trust yourself. Trusting yourself means that you;

1) Maintain consciousness as much as possible; be a student of your self, a non-judgmental observer of your self, stay connected with your self and be present in every moment.

2) Remember that there is nothing wrong with you; you are in good working order. What needs to be fixed is the idea that you need fixed.

3) Know that masculinity is inherently good and designed to benefit the world.

Reflection Questions

Make an assessment of how free you feel in life. From 0 to 10, how free do you feel? Generally? With work? In relationships? Spiritually?

So far in your life, what has kept you from fully trusting yourself?

How Alert and Oriented (AOx4) do you feel in your life? Do you know who you are, where your are, what time it is, and what is happening?

What are your clues that you are asleep in your own life, oblivious to what is going on?

How much influence does it feel like you have in your own world?

What has kept you from observing yourself?

How might you start to eliminate self-criticism in your life?

How have you struggled with disconnection or compartmentalizing?

How could you become more connected with yourself?

What do you need to do to be able to see your "failures" as good feedback for learning?

How has the past and the future kept you from the present?

What could you do today to live in the present more profoundly?

What's on your list of what's wrong with you?

Let your imagination go for a moment; what would happen if everyone on the planet lived from their heart?

What needs to happen for you to move forward and believe you have the goods?

What messages have you heard about the value of masculinity?

How have you been confused about the strength of your masculinity?

How could you begin moving forward in life using your masculinity as an internal resource?

Solid Challenge #8: Consciousness

The last challenge was about checking in. Checking in is the start to a life of conscious awareness. Consciousness is defined as being awake and aware in your life.

Many of us have just been going through the motions and living as others have expected. It is really living the 'blue pill' life where there is something going on, but there is no awareness or understanding of what that is. Living this unobservant or oblivious lifestyle is what has caused much of the pain you have experienced. It also is what causes powerlessness and lack of influence. It is time to wake up.

This is counter intuitive, but the first step to waking up to what's happening around you requires that you start to become attentive to what is going on inside of you. All the tools you ever needed to figure life out are all ready to go in you. You just need to listen to them. That's what the rest of this book is all about. But first you need to make sure you are starting to come out of your slumber.

How deep asleep do you think you have been? In what ways would you say you have been oblivious?

We will talk more about looking to the internals, but up to this point how adept have you been with checking in with yourself and knowing what is going on in your body, with your emotions and in your spirit?

Some people call this concept mindfulness, others call it contemplative living. Whatever you call it, it is just about letting yourself see what is going on inside of you and from there gaining a greater understanding of what is happening outside of you as well.

Our narrative of what is happening outside of us usually comes from what others have told us. We have heard from parents, teachers, pastors and other influential people what life is all about, what values are valuable and what is truth. I want you to challenge all of that and start to define life by what you are really seeing.

You probably already know the truth about life but have been restraining it forever. To build awareness you must allow yourself to accept what you know to be true.

What are some truths you have been avoiding? (Consider things like; the work I am doing isn't right for me, my relationship is stagnant, or something needs to change with drinking, eating, lifestyle, etc.) **Just say the truth and write it down, accept it.**

Imagine that your world is just like Neo's from _The Matrix_. There is something else going on that you are totally unaware of. Imagine a great conspiracy that exists in the life you are living right now, describe it here. **What does it look like? What is your role?**

Often, people need a crisis or critical event in life to wake up to the realities in life. Things like losing a job or marriage difficulties are like a slap in the face or 2x4 across the temple. Sometimes it is like Neo, where something very subtle gets your attention. **What crises or subtle clues have been waking you up to awareness that there is something bigger going on? What does that "bigger thing" look like?**

We don't have to wait for a crisis to happen to become aware and awake. This can actually become a way of living. Checking in is a great first step. But more intention is needed. You've already been this way before, but you lost it. **What have you done in the past that has helped you keep focused, centered or awake?**

What are three things you could be doing every day to keep yourself more centered, awake and intentionally engaged with life?

1.

2.

3.

7 THE SHADOW SELF

We've already looked at how we often think we are broken or something in us needs to be fixed and that nothing needs fixed. But we still have more floating around in us that needs some explanation.

We all know we have a side to us that seems to be the "bad" part of us. I call this part of us the Shadow Self. The Shadow Self is not evidence that something is wrong with us. It's not our core or our true self, it is just a shadow of our true self which is trying to fix our problems in foolish ways.

The Shadow Self is very similar to our "False Self" in that it is just a part of us that is hanging around the perimeter of our lives; neither of them are your True Self. The False Self is the imagined identity that we have come to believe about who we are and where we gain our value and acceptance. The Shadow Self is who we are when we forget our True Self and when we let externals drive us or define us.

☞ **The Shadow Self is who we are when we live foolishly.**

The Shadow Self comes alive when we try to solve our problems or reduce our anxiety and fear by taking pathways of foolish behavior. This is when we rely on externals to fill in the gaps in our life. It is when we blame externals for our problems by taking a victim posture.

When we try desperately to resolve our inner conflicts through external things is where things get ugly. All our problems come from our attempts to resolve core difficulties in our life, externally. In our desperation we are actually trying to find our Source, but we take pathways where we always fall short.

The existence of the Shadow Self is just evidence that often we move and choose to live life in very foolish ways, not that we are broken. In the journey to trust your internals we must become proficient at identifying your Shadow Self and not allowing it to run the show.

I'll use the account of Adam and Eve to illustrate this. Most people would agree that at the start Adam and Eve were free of shame and nothing was wrong with them, they were perfect. Yet, when they were deceived, they chose to believe that they needed something external of themselves to be complete. They believed that God was keeping something from them.

So they chose to eat the fruit from the Tree of Knowledge of Good and Evil. They then experienced shame (something needed to be hidden) and separation from God. We make these same kind of choices every day and we experience similar consequences as well.

The Shadow Self came out in their confusion, silence and faulty belief that there was something more. If two people who were perfect can fall to the Shadow Self, we are obviously susceptible as well.

We must understand that our foolish choices don't come from a flawed core, but from our beliefs about life.

◌ The Shadow Self reveals our true beliefs.

What we believe about life and our Source of life is what drives our decisions. We are just like Adam and Eve when we are deceived to believe lies about needing externals to complete us or make us acceptable.

The Shadow Self reveals itself in our lives when we are deceived about who we really are and what really brings us life.

The realm of our beliefs is a central category in the journey to become solid. If you believe the lies or false narratives about who you are, what you need to be whole or acceptable and where you think true life comes from, you will fall into an external reference and allow the Shadow Self to run your life.

If you reject the lies and begin to live by the true narrative, you will live in freedom. Jesus said it like this to people who were following him, "You will know the truth, and the truth will set you free!" Once you are able to live by the truth about who you really are, you can truly live life in freedom.

Indicators

We all have our own set of behaviors or postures that are indicators of the presence of the Shadow Self. The following list will help you identify when the Shadow Self is leading your life.

Just like the previous long lists, read them slowly and out-loud. Then circle the ones that have been your way of living.

judgmental	dishonest
whiny	disengaged
defensive	depressed
manipulative	boastful
abusive	violent
demanding	arrogant
controlling	compartmentalized
avoidant	worrying
withdrawn	not centered
addicted	unconscious
explosive	intimidating
silenced or silent	bullying
passive	pushy
impulsive	fault-finding
compulsive	conceding too often
obsessive	pleasing
procrastinating	cold-shoulder
blaming	dismissive

minimizing	deflecting
lacking self-control	never wrong
hyper-focused	sarcastic
hard-hearted	unreliable
butt hurt	shamed
fixated	critical
hopeless	deflated
given up or given in	accusatory
frustrated	grumpy
impatient	confused
passive-aggressive	forgetful
victimhood	unbelief
tyrannical	self-doubt
pity-party	disrespectful
throwing a tantrum	forcing it
distracted	anxious

It seems that this may be a list of defining characteristics of who we are, but these are not definers. While the Shadow Self is you moving in a certain way and believing certain things, it is not who you are.

For me my main indicators that the Shadow Self is running the show is when I get this passive and withdrawn posture. Sometimes it looks whiny or even like a tantrum, it is very subtle. Then every once in a while there is an explosion if the energy builds up enough. It's been like I am a volcano and the pressure is getting ready to erupt. It's very passive-aggressive.

The more I check in and become aware of what is deeper in me, I have begun to identify what I am believing, what I'm afraid of and what the Shadow Self is trying to do.

Key Components

Remember that the Shadow Self is what your good heart looks like **when you forget** to live from internals and when you allow externals to run the show. The problem is that you forget who you are and become driven by externals.

> ⟳ **The Shadow Self comes alive when we are unconscious, fearful, self-protective, externally-referenced, forgetful and dis-integrated.**

Let's take a closer look at those parts of the Shadow Self.

Unconscious; This happens when we live in our head and stop paying attention to our internal resources. We are unconscious when we fall "asleep", when we are oblivious, unaware or withdrawn. We've already talked about how important it is to maintain consciousness at all times in your life. When we lose consciousness the Shadow Self rules your life and I allow my old roles to act in default mode.

Fearful; Fear is a huge enemy to the integrated man. Fear can shut us down and lock us up. You must know that you can handle whatever comes your way. Acknowledge your fear and courageously move into whatever is fearful.

Fear is not evidence of inadequacy. Fear is an indicator that something significant is going on. Fear is meant to be challenged so you can actually challenge your beliefs about life. Unconscious fear is at the heart of the Shadow Self.

Self-protective; Masculinity is designed to protect, to use your power for others around you. When we get self-protective and defensive our masculinity shrivels and our lives become small. It is true that we must have strong boundaries for how people treat us, but true strength is seen in a man who does not have to defend himself.

Through self-protection we will get controlling or withdrawn; either way it creates unhealthy patterns. We can get defensive and try to explain our way out of situations, rather than take ownership for them. Self-protection exists when life is shriveled in upon itself; that's what the Shadow Self looks like.

Externally-referenced; This is when everything outside of you runs the show or defines who you are. Things are turned outside-in and we are driven by an external "matrix" which controls us.

This false life is the Shadow Self life; there is no true substance or vitality to it.

The Shadow Self thrives in the world of the externally referenced life. There is actually no other option; the externally referenced self actually is the Shadow Self.

Forgetting; When we forget, we believe the lies about who we are and where our value comes from. We are shame-based when we believe we are a mistake and we are broken. We believe the False Narratives that we are not good enough or we don't have what it takes.

We allow the Shadow Self to thrive when we forget who we are, where our true source of life is or when we believe we have no control over our own lives.

Dis-integrated; When we are internally separated from important parts of ourselves we are dis-integrated. This is when we don't listen to our heart or our body. It is not holistically integrating all your parts. "Dualism" is thinking some parts of you are less important or valuable, then disregarding their impact.

A definition of Hell often is centered on the word "separation". Hell is separation from God, from others and most profoundly from yourself. The dis-integrated man is in a "living hell"; the Shadow Self escorts you there.

The concept of separation is significant here since most people carry some angst from feeling alone or not acceptable. With this inner turmoil we will do some incredibly foolish things to try to feel accepted and loved. This is the Shadow Self trying to make things work. But it doesn't work to live from this place.

The Flesh

The Bible calls this part of you "The Flesh". The Flesh is not referring to our physical flesh or body, but a way of living that sets itself against the spirit or internal parts of us. "The Flesh" has a way of running the show when we are living in fear, forgetting or self-protection. It works its way into our lives when we forget where life really comes from and when we pursue counterfeits to feel better or escape difficulties.

➔ **The Bible concept of the "Flesh" is the Shadow Self.**

"Since the Shadow Self or the Flesh is part of my inner world it seems that there is something wrong with me. I actually have a deep desire to do what is right and good with my life, but sometimes it seems like the Shadow Self is too strong. When I let the Shadow Self run the show I end up not doing the good things that my good heart wants to do. So this is where it feels like something bad is in me, since often I have a difficult time doing what my good heart wants to do; it's as though something else in me is directing my steps to move foolishly. Whenever I want to do what is good and right, there is always a choice to act foolishly, against what is right. Even though inside my heart I am excited to do good and accomplish great things, I experience a kind of battle that messes with my mind. My mind starts to believe the lies and that's when I get sucked into the bondage of the Shadow Self. That's when I feel like I really suck and wonder if I will ever be free." (Paraphrase of Romans 7:15-24)

For me, I have realized that gaining freedom has been a teamwork effort. I am a follower of Jesus and I believe that somehow through what he has accomplished, I am free. I also believe that he has dealt with all my questions about my acceptance and value. So, I don't have to be perfect and I can rest. I also believe that he wants me to live freely, which means he wants me to trust the good heart he has given me. He enjoys watching me move freely as I go through life. Teamwork means that he has made my freedom possible and my work is to live in that freedom.

Freedom will always be elusive if you do not identify the battlefield. The battle is not against you or your own soul. When wrestling with the Shadow Self, the battle is in the realm of your beliefs; where do I believe life comes from and who do I believe I am.

When you forget the true answers to those questions, you will fall into the clutches of the Shadow Self and your behaviors will turn toward folly and sin.

Restraining the Shadow Self

As we interact with the Shadow Self we must remember that we have complete responsibility. We have control over our decisions and ownership of all our actions. It may seem at times that the Shadow Self takes on a life of its own taking us for a ride which feels powerless, but we do have control. To live a solid life of integrity, you must become proficient at understanding and restraining your own Shadow Self.

Some people actually have names for their Shadow Self; the Dragon, the Beast, the Bear, Jack-ass, the Vulture, the Dick, the Weasel, Lieutenant Dike; you may have a name for it as well. If not, give it a personalized name so you can identify it, because it is yours.

My boys would say something like "Release the Beast" when I would get emotionally out of control. That was my Shadow Self taking control. I also have a tendency to get quiet and clam up. This has been my main self-protection mechanism. Mine is the Beast that will hide in silence and then every once in a while, explode.

We must learn to purposely put the Shadow Self into a cage, where it has no power over you. The Shadow Self will always be present in your life, it just does not have to be your friend, define you or have control over anything.

The Shadow Self will try to elbow its way into your life by disguising itself as an internal resource. It might look like an instinct, intuition or even a spiritual concept. It can be despicable like that. Keep your eyes open and you'll get good at identifying when the Shadow Self cuts in.

The internally referenced life seeks abundance and thriving in life. The Shadow Self lives in scarcity and deprivation. The Shadow Self lives in fear and is just trying to keep you safe. But scarcity and self-protection always limit you from moving forward in strength and confidence.

When you sense something holding you back or when you are not able to live fully, observe to see if it is the Shadow Self. The Shadow Self keeps you from a full life of vitality.

A very significant concept in the Solid Man process is living from your heart. You will learn to trust your heart and follow how it leads you every moment of your life. You will learn to be conscious and aware of the state of your heart as you move through life. This conscious awareness will be one of your greatest tools to keeping check on the Shadow Self.

The Shadow Self thrives when the heart is hard or closed off. Hard-heartedness is a sign that the Shadow Self is alive and well. Take time to check in with your heart and do everything to live with an open heart at all times.

Awareness of your Shadow Self is essential as you learn to move in strength and freedom. Know what your Shadow Self looks like and remember that it is not your core. When you notice the Shadow Self running the show, regroup and get your solidness back.

There are many indicators that the Shadow Self is not running the show. This is when you are playful, inquisitive, centered, content and free. It is as though you have a childlike posture and you are enjoying life. You will begin to experience many definers of a Shadow Self free life.

The Cherokee legend of the Two Wolves simply illustrates the internal battle.

> An old Cherokee is teaching his grandson about life. "A fight is going on inside me," he said to the boy. "It is a terrible fight and it is between two wolves. One is evil - he is anger, envy, sorrow, regret, greed, arrogance, self-pity, guilt, resentment, inferiority, lies, false pride, superiority, and ego."

> He continued, "The other is good - he is joy, peace, love, hope, serenity, humility, kindness, benevolence, empathy, generosity, truth, compassion, and faith. The same fight is going on inside you - and inside every other person, too."

> The grandson thought about it for a minute and then asked his grandfather, "Which wolf will win?" The old Cherokee simply replied, "The one you feed."

So it is with the Shadow Self. If we continue to give it front row in the decisions of our life, it will determine the path we follow.

⮱ **Shadow Self Directive –**

Stay conscious and aware of how the Shadow Self comes alive in your life. When it raises its ugly head, notice it and regroup to your internals.

Reflection Questions

Which indicators of the Shadow Self come alive in you most?

Of the six major parts of the Shadow Self - Unconscious, Fearful, Self-protective, Externally-referenced, Forgetting, or Dis-integrated; Which of these have been the ways the Shadow Self exists in your life? How so?

What have you heard about yourself and what causes "sin" in your life?

How do you think the battle for your soul is in the realm of your beliefs?

In what ways have you kept yourself from responsibility, as though you did not choose or we not at fault?

What name have you given or called your Shadow Self?

What have you done in the past to allow yourself to open your heart and be more vulnerable?

What has happened when you have fed the beast? Or not?

How has the Shadow Self disguised itself as a positive internal resource?

In what ways have you experienced the Shadow Self in your life?

What could you do right now to limit its influence over you?

Solid Challenge #9: Keeping an Open Heart

This challenge is all about your heart. There are times when our hearts are open and there are times when it is closed. Often you can actually sense when something happens and your heart becomes closed or opens up. Since this happens without choice, just take it as it is, your heart opening or closing just happens.

For this challenge you will need to begin to pay attention to yourself in a very active fashion. Be very honest and open about what is really happening in your heart. You'll get better with time and practice. You find you are actually better at this than you realize.

As you move through your day and interact with people, watch how you heart becomes open or closed. When your heart becomes open you feel warm toward someone, supported, alive, connected, affirmed, positive, more willing to serve, safe, desired, playful, passionate, engaged, willing, attraction, confident, and any number of things like this. Your body will actually look open; your posture and face will be open turning towards someone. When your heart becomes closed you will feel cold to others, distant, alone, belittled, small, vulnerable, rejected, unwilling, negative, deflated, withdrawn and a number of other things like this. Your body will be closed; crossed legs or arms, facial expressions, turned away from others and other non-verbals show a closed heart. Each one of us reacts to stimuli differently, what closes one person may not bother someone else.

The challenge is to make two lists. 20 things that open your heart. and 20 things that close your heart. Here are some examples to help you out.

Heart Opener Examples: My heart opens with a smile, laughter, flirting, kindness appreciation, affection, you say you are wrong, unexpected sex, you listen, etc.

Your 20 Openers:

Heart Closer Examples: My heart closes with sarcasm, raised voices, silent treatment, I feel forgotten, I get 'the look', rejection, shame, blame, belittled, etc.

Your 20 Closers:

Make this the language you use in life. "My heart feels very closed right now, I need some space", "What you did last night after dinner really opened up my heart", "You look like your heart just closed, what is that like for you?". Be aware of when you close off or open up, talk about it when it happens. **When have you experienced having a hard or closed heart?**

8 YOUR INTERNAL RESOURCES

⮫ **To be a solid, integrated, masculine man, you must have an internal point of reference.**

The life of a Solid Man is motivated and expressed from the realities inside his being. These inner realities have depth, substance, and structure which define his character and essence.

Since we have been trained to disregard our inner workings, we don't follow the guidance we receive from inside us. There is a "disconnect" inside of us. This chapter will outline significant aspects of our brilliant inner workings to give you some concrete pathways to begin your journey of listening to and following your Internal Resources.

⮫ **We have lost the fine art of listening to ourselves.**

When considering how we have been built, the idea of Dualism is often a defining factor. Dualism is the belief that there are two parts of the human, usually one part higher and the other part lower or less valuable. For instance, because of how dualism has influenced philosophy and theology, our sexual or physical parts have been seen as less important than the spiritual or intellectual. The physical is base or perverse and the spiritual or intellectual is sacred and more valuable.

Dualism creates a dichotomy which eliminates the capacity to respect and honor all parts of our inner workings. The Solid Man Process seeks to eliminate Dualism in all its forms so we can be free to trust and regard **all** parts of our being.

This holistic foundation sees humans as whole and complete. This is also "non-pathological" in that this process is not looking to find out what is wrong with you but is based on the fact that you have good inner resources already in you.

So many theories about people and relationships today are based in pathological thought that something is wrong with you. The passion to these "professionals" is to find what needs to be fixed or what pill will eliminate the symptom. I'm sure you have experienced this somehow.

The primary Internal Resources that I will be outlining are your Wisdom, Heart, Soul, Mind and Strength. While there are many ways to explain or teach the various aspects of who we are as humans, for clarity, I have chosen these primary aspects as important to this process.

The goal of this process is to recover your ability to listen to and follow your core internals. This process can become overly complex; my goal is to be as simple as possible so it will be easier to understand, so you can begin to master the art of listening to yourself.

    ☞ **Remember to Check In.**

Wisdom, the Real Boss

Integration of your internal processes develops wisdom. Wisdom increases through gathering vital information in order to make good choices. Wisdom is gained through experience as you take in knowledge and common sense in order to create positive outcomes in your life.

    ☞ **A smart man learns from his mistakes. A wise man learns from other's mistakes.**

Wisdom embodies life. It encapsulates our intellect, common sense, action, and our intention. You know wisdom when you see it. True wisdom resonates with your soul and feels right. Wisdom often has a sense of ancient depth. It has been carried through from one generation to the next in unexplainable ways. People and communities carry wisdom in their midst. Wisdom is a relational, spiritual, and intellectual process of knowing the right way to move.

Wisdom incorporates all aspects of internal process and translates it into action and movement. Wisdom is the main process of the internally referenced life. Wisdom is what we will seek as we listen to our core internals for the purpose of living a good life of freedom.

114

Wisdom often comes packaged as common sense, or the ability to have good judgement in practical matters. Common sense often seems to flow from your internal intuitive process. It seems the more you have to think about something, the less common sense is there.

Gather as much earthly and spiritual wisdom as you can and lock it into your internal grid. Wisdom will come to you from the Scriptures, wise people, metaphor, science, observing the world, listening, good stories, experience, just about anywhere.

⋄ **When you see true wisdom, embrace it; don't let go.**

Use the wisdom you gather for action that increases your well-being and for the benefit of everyone around you. Wisdom will guide you to develop a strong life. When you find it, keep hold of it deeply within you.

This is what is meant in the Psalms when the poet says to God, "Your word I have hid in my heart that I will not sin against you." He takes the wisdom and understanding from the words God has given him into his deep internal resources to guide and direct his choices. Allowing deep truths of life to "lock in" to your internal matrix is essential as you move through life.

Wisdom is much more than knowing something, it couples physical, emotional and spiritual parts of us; parts that experience life, develop competencies, express power and move with intention. Wisdom is designed to be the authority in your life. If you let wisdom rule, you will do just fine.

⊠ **Wisdom = Optimum Judgment for Optimum Action**

Wisdom is developed through judging. Humans are in the process of judging almost every moment of every day. We are forming opinions or evaluations all the time about whether a situation is safe, what a person said is true, or if a course of action is best.

Wisdom is shaped by the skilled ability to see, observe and discern what is right and true. From there the goal of wisdom is the best possible action with the best possible outcome.

Folly is the opposite of wisdom, poor judgment which makes poor action. Folly is ignoring important information. It is having weak judgment which results in foolish action. Folly is well represented by the externally referenced life. We keep Folly around by ignoring internal processes which give us vital wisdom-developing information.

Since you cannot escape your beliefs in life, your beliefs are embodied in your folly. What you believe reveals your actions and decisions in life. The beliefs that keep you enslaved are often called toxic beliefs or as Dr. Robert Glover refers to them, self-limiting beliefs (SLB's). Challenging your long held toxic beliefs and gaining true wisdom is your path to integrity and freedom.

You have seen and experienced folly in your life and in your actions. Up to this point you've been highly externally referenced and wisdom may have bypassed you often. Notice how your present beliefs have restrained you and kept you from living in freedom. It is time to reclaim your wisdom by believing the truth.

> ◔ *The glory of young men is their strength, but the glory of old men is their gray hair (wisdom)*   *- Proverbs*

Since Wisdom is central to living an internally referenced life, your goal is to gather prime information from your internal resources and then make life decisions for the best course of action. Wisdom is designed to be the master or the boss.

> ◔ **With Wisdom at the helm, you will do just fine.**

When other things run the show like Externals, the Shadow Self, or even the Mind, things will go bad, quickly. Nothing else has the goods to run the show. Wisdom is one of your best parts so hold on tight.

<u>**Wisdom Directive –**</u>

Seek the optimum action for every decision in your life.

In what ways have you been taught to trust your internal resources? Or not?

In what ways have you seen folly connected to external reference?

Wisdom is simply Optimum Judgment for Optimum Action how can you begin to implement the intentional pursuit of wisdom in your life? Or how could you build yourself into a wisdom producing machine?

The Mind; the Interpreter

In our world today, we have not been taught the value of our internal processes, let alone the value of integrating them fully into our daily lives. We usually diminish our emotions, intuition, instincts, anxieties, failures and fears instead of using them as valuable sources of information through which to thrive.

In the present world we've been taught to live primarily in the rational and cognitive with the mind. Our mind is a great resource, but without integrating the rest of you, your mental processes always become imbalanced and overbearing. So many men get caught up in their heads with analysis – paralysis.

Western culture has been highly influenced by "Modernity" for the past century. Modernity placed a very high value on the mind and what is known. Modern Western science and philosophy has seen knowledge and intellect as the most valuable human asset.

Since we live in these times, we all have been taught from the great scientists and philosophers from the Modern age. It is what science, theology and academics have been built upon for the past century or so. The mind has been the king in the Modern world.

> ➔ **"I think, therefore I am." is a very limited view of a human, there is so much more.**

Modernists sought to cypher all the mysteries of the ages, from the origin of species to the nature of man and then present their findings into a nice little box with a bow on it. The goal was to figure it all out and know all the answers to the universe. Darwin, Marx, Nietzsche and Freud all gave a strong attempt to explain the world, each of their own field of study.

Now with the rise of quantum physics and so many other scientific findings, more questions than answers have arisen. Mystery is embraced more often in what is now becoming the Post-modern world.

You have been baptized into the Modern worldview whether you know it or not. Now, in order to become integrated and internally referenced, you must break free from the idea that your mind is king. Or that you can figure it out.

Here is the real truth about the mind; the mind is designed for interpretation, consciousness and awareness, it has **not** been made for running the show.

➔ **As a servant, the mind is magnificent; as a master, it is despotic.**

There is so much more to be experienced than what is thought. Trying to figure life out throws you into a vortex of futility which results in frustration and angst. The mind likes certainty, so when there is mystery or uncertainty, the mind gets really uncomfortable. Since becoming more comfortable with uncertainty is required in order to live in the present with confidence, you must allow the mind to do its real job – which is to serve the process and not to lead the process.

➔ **You don't have to figure it all out to get it right, just listen in real time.**

As a servant your mind is an awesome part of your internal information gathering system. It cannot be the master or the controller. The perfect role of the mind is to gather information about what is going on and help process that information.

In order to develop Wisdom, the Mind takes information from your core, from your surroundings, and your knowledge, then interprets what is happening and then chooses the best course of action. Then the Body carries out the plan. The Mind, Heart and Body are designed to work together as a well-oiled machine, creating a life of power and freedom.

I am describing integration of all your being in full collaboration; all parts working as one. The mind is part of that process. Mindfulness means you are aware, conscious and "checking in" with your Self in real time.

➔ **Check-in with yourself - Often.**

The mindful check-in is just asking yourself what is going on or what is happening right now. Often it is just recognizing a feeling or experience and wondering what it is. Conscious checking in with your internal resources is essential to gathering vital information so you can live from the inside-out.

Checking in with your internals helps you to find your center. Your center is that core place inside of you that interacts with life and interfaces with all of your experience. Finding your center is just about finding you.

Since we have often been trained to disregard ourselves to keep others happy, checking in with yourself or finding your center may sound selfish or even narcissistic. While it is introspective, this is not selfish. I like to call it selfness.

Remember your life is about you, so live from the center of you. Where else would we live from, someone else's center? This is your life; it has been designed to be lived from the inside-out.

> ➔ **Your life actually is all about you. So be you, unapologetically.**

Finding your center also has to do with finding your Source and connecting on a consistent basis. The Source is that place where "Life" comes from. We will talk more about your Source and your Daily Practice in lessons to come.

As we develop a strong internally referenced life and as we connect intentionally with our Source we will be able to move expansively into our relationships with wisdom and love.

Your Mind gathers information by asking questions in the present; "how am I doing?", "What is going on here?", "This doesn't seem right.", "Why is my heart racing?" or "How can I move with integrity right now?" The Mind will help to create the best choice or course of action.

> ➔ **The Mind gathers and interprets information from your internals.**

When the Mind adds information that is old (not from the present), from a preconceived experience or when it's influenced by the Shadow Self is when the Mind makes things a little nutsy.

You'll be thinking about a fear from something that happened when you were a kid or when shame made you second guess yourself. "Remember what happened at the barn?" or "You really think you can do this right this time?" This outside information adds confusion to the work of the mind.

The Mind is actually trying to protect you, but it is using out of date info and adding fears/shame/doubts to the mix. You must use good present information from internal resources and your deep well of wisdom to decide what to do next. The Mind gathers that information like a champ. Don't let it divert you to old stuff.

Your Mind is your tool to discern the good information which comes from your center. Mindfulness is checking-in with yourself and then taking the information about what is going on inside of you to create wise avenues of movement and action.

Mind Directive –

Use your Mind to gather information and to discern optimum action, not to run the show.

In what ways do you get stuck in your head?

In what ways do you try to figure things out?

What could you do to Check-in mindfully more often?

Your Core; the Heart of All Things

Your Core is central to how you gather wisdom in your life. Your Core brings together the integration of all your internal parts working together. We often use the metaphor of the heart to refer to our Core or our essential being. Whatever you call it, your Heart or your Core, it is your center. To live in strength and freedom, you must fully engage with the central parts of you.

> ⊙ **The answer is closer than we have been led to believe. God has given us a road map for the life each of us is meant to live. But the map is contained in a place we seldom go - our hearts.** **Gary Barkalow**

People describe having an open heart or times when their heart is closed or hard. Awareness of the state of your heart is important to doing this process well. You must become aware of when your heart is closed or hard, when it is open and vulnerable. You must know the experiences that create the conditions that open or close your heart.

> ⊙ **At all costs, live with an OPEN heart.**

To become the man you want to be and to eliminate the problems you have in your life, you must become intimately connected to your own heart, to your own state of being.

Your Core is primary to everything you do and brings all of who you are together. Some say it is your spiritual center as well.

You will master your life as you become able to observe yourself and how you move. Mastery develops in you as you are able to notice your inner workings and how you interact with the world. Remember, don't judge yourself, just notice what you are feeling, experiencing and what your heart is telling you.

> ☞ **The Heart is the interface with the deep realities of existence.**

The word "heart" is used to describe your center, or the internal parts of you that are deeply "moved" at times with happiness, energy, passion or grief. Some cultures use the "liver", "kidneys" or often "bowels" to refer to the center. Others will call these deep places your "spirit" or your "soul".

Whatever you call it the point is this, to awaken your internals you must live from your heart, your center or whatever is at your core. As cheesy as "follow your heart" may sound, connection to your heart is absolutely essential if you are to live in freedom.

> ☞ **The Heart is the crossroads of the internally referenced life.**

Living by externals makes us feel like we can't get it right. As though I need to figure out the riddle or find the code. But life is not lived by an equation; there is no code or secret. Life is lived by listening to your Heart.

People love the certainty of equations so we can figure out how to make life work. Most religions, parents and therapists try to develop some pattern that will lead the way; $A + B = C$. It would be something like; Follow Rules + Don't Do Wrong Things = Good Things (Acceptance and Belonging). It is some equation that fixes things.

The fact is that no equation ever resulted in freedom. Actually, the opposite is true, you become enslaved by equations. The equations become a book of rules/laws designed to govern your life, to try to help you get it right. You believe that if you follow the rules to the "T" then you will gain the acceptance you want. This always ends badly, because somewhere along the way your heart "dies" into a passionless existence as you try to follow some list of external rules.

> ☞ **Success and strength in life does not come from a secret code, it does come from following your good internal resources, they will guide you well.**

The challenge is to live from your Core, what can you do to be more centered and mindful of your deep internal parts?

When is the best time for you to check-in to observe yourself?

Often, we live by an equation like this; Follow Rules + Don't Do Wrong Things = Good Things (Acceptance and Belonging). What has your life equation been?

How has that worked for you, or what have been the consequences?

<u>Core Directive</u> –

Live with a conscious, open heart, by listening to all your Internal Resources.

6 Categories of Your Internal Resources

Your Internal Resources

This graphic represents all your Internal Resources that you have available to help you move intentionally toward Wisdom. Let's look at all the parts and sub-parts that are ours to use.

Heart, Soul, Mind, Strength, Laws/Responsibilities & the Dark Side

In Mark 12:30, Jesus teaches us to love God with all our Heart, Soul, Mind and Strength. He is encouraging us to use all of our being to love God. I am using this as a way to categorize our internal resources. Tons of people do this either saying there are two parts, three parts, four parts or many parts to a human being. You have to come down somewhere in order to explain this, so these are aspects of a man's being I identify that are designed to guide and direct his life and actions.

Regardless, the point is to know that Internal Resources are very important to observe with integration, where it all works together. Some of us compartmentalize, where we stay away from parts we see as scary, weak or not worthwhile. That is a pathway to foolishness, all your parts need attention. Integration is our goal and the simple act of "Checking In" is our practice to keep all parts integrated.

Heart - "That Which Moves"

The Heart is that part of us that moves. It is the part that connects with things and people, knows without knowing, feels deeply, feels in nuanced ways and sees beyond what is here. The Heart is what is moved when you see a good movie or hear a good story. It is what grieves when you hear of the death of a friend. It is what you feel when you sense somethings not quite right with a situation. It is the way a good joke comes out of nowhere. It is the sense of awe when you see something beautiful, like a sunset, your baby being born or your wife's naked body.

The Heart has been much aligned in many contexts. The church often sees the Heart as despicable and misleading. Children's movies of often say "follow your heart" which then is criticized as being illogical or childlike. Women are told to follow their intuition, but men are not since it is not logical. It is true that the Heart is not exactly logical and sometimes doesn't even make sense, but it is still one of the most valuable parts of our internal resources.

All the resources are incredibly important, so we must never disregard our Heart. Here are the parts of the Heart that we have so we can live full and abundant lives.

Intuitive; Gut, Humor, Instinctive, 6th sense, "Blink"

Passion; Emotions, Desire, Wants, Well-being, Love, Compassion, Empathy, Sacrifice

Spirit; Faith, Beliefs, Worship, Connection w/the Divine or Source, Transcendence

Heart Directive –

- Live with a conscious, open heart, by listening to all your Internal Resources.

Intuition

For men, intuition has also been diminished in profound ways. Women's intuition is thought of as legendary. Men's intuition is just as real and valid; we have been trained to disregard it.

Just like emotions, men are equally as intuitive as women. Intuition is the ability to understand something immediately, without the need for conscious reasoning. Intuition feels like some kind of secret knowledge that just comes to you; you know without knowing. You may not know the details of what is going on, but you know something is at play.

Intuition has been called many things; blink, instinct, gut, or a 6th sense. Whatever you call it, your intuition is astonishingly brilliant. Intuition is connected to something transcendent, something beyond us, yet in us.

Intuition can make quick judgments that are spot on. We must allow our intuitive to become a significant part of our internal information gathering system if we are to live in freedom and strength.

Intuition is expressed well in a good timed joke with friends. You sense what to say, you let it go and everyone laughs. If you hesitate to filter it or wait for a good moment, it usually will fall flat. Humor is intuitive and flows from that internal place. Humor is one of my favorite internal resources. Laughter is a significant gift of life in so many ways. Allowing humor to be an internal resource of the heart is fun, playful and life-giving. Set your humor free to be a strong internal resource.

How have you interacted with intuition in your life? Disregarded it, followed it, and what happened when you did either of these?

Passion

We usually think of passion as emotion, dreams and purpose. These words accurately describe passion. Passion is about wanting and desire. It is about a deep experience of longing as you desire something you don't have.

Passion also has to do with sacrifice and emptiness, as with "The Passion of the Christ". Passion is the discipline of going without something you desire. The two concepts of desire and emptiness embody passion.

Passion is usually equated with lust. Lust is the demand that desire must be gratified. Lust cannot handle the emptiness of true desire. The entire porn industry has the illusion of passion, but it only lust. Lust is shallow and small. Lust misses the richness of what true passion provides.

Desire in its true form is emptiness or not having something. Emptiness is actually what defines desire. Desire no longer exists as soon as you have what you desire. Passion and desire embody the experience of wanting something without the demand for satiation. A man of Passion pursues what he desires vigorously, however, he is also able to maturely delay his gratification as he moves with wisdom.

☞ Passion walking with Wisdom is Maturity

Passion is expressed most significantly in our emotions. The emotional aspects of your life have to do with what you are feeling or experiencing at any given moment; moods, feelings, anxieties, fears, etc.... Emotions reveal what you want. Emotions indicate what you need so you can be responsible to make sure your needs are met. Emotions give you significant clues about what is going on in you and around you.

Emotions are not designed to run the show, they are designed to give you valuable information about what you want, what you need to do next and to guide you to be responsible to care for yourself and others.

☞ Your emotions rationally make sense.

You may be questioning this concept as you read this. Take some time with this and let it sink in. You have been sold a bill of goods that emotions are irrational, feminine, untamed or an obstacle to effective living.

Integrating emotions fully into your life is essential and absolutely necessary to living a fully masculine life. Men are equally as emotional as women; it is part of being human. Men just do emotions differently. Chip Dodd said emotions are the "voice" of the heart. To care for yourself, you must listen to your emotions. They guide you to what you want and need.

Your emotional process guides you toward increasing your sense of well-being. When you are angry it is always for a reason. It is because your well-being has been diminished and you need something in order to thrive.

☞ Emotions always reveal our well-being and help us to get it back.

Not listening to our emotional process is where we fall into horrible patterns of developing external soothers in our life. As we disregard the information emotions give us we often seek some thing outside of us to soothe those difficult emotions. We choose all kinds of things to self-medicate or to escape tough feelings.

We also try to get everything in control, so we do everything we can to manipulate or control things outside of us to feel like we have power in our life. This dead-end way of life always results in anxiety and frustration because you only can control yourself.

Later in this process we will learn how to fully integrate your emotions into creating a full and thriving life. For now, begin to notice and experience how emotions are a significant part of your internal resources.

Remember passion is also sacrifice and emptiness. The maturity of a Solid Man actually is developed in the process of delayed gratification or going without something. Purposefully choosing to go without something is understanding that even though it may be important to help you thrive, you can go without it for a season.

> ◌ **Maturity is living in the balance of emptiness and desire.**

Embracing the emptiness of passion creates maturity and mastery in your life. Living in the emptiness of not having something is actually living in the desire. You would no longer desire it, if you had it. Passion is another vital internal resource that we must listen to daily.

Our life has a bigger purpose and higher calling. We often use all our energy dealing with shame, trying to blame others and fighting with our own selves. We came into this world with a greater calling and mission.

As you develop a stronger identity you will be able to listen to your passions or what makes your heart come alive. This process will help to unveil your purpose and gaining clarity on your higher purpose is important to being a Solid Man.

How have you diminished your emotional life?

In what ways can you listen to your emotions more?

How could Passion be a strong guide in your life?

Spirit

Spirituality is that part of you that is connected with the unseen or mysterious parts of life. It is the arena of things that are sacred, of faith and worship. Faith is believing something that is unseen or uncertain. Worship is pursuing something that you believe will bring you "life", fulfillment or wholeness.

Your spirit is that part of you that connects to those unclear and unknown aspects of living. It is that part of you that experiences the sacred parts of life that seem to come from some transcendent place. Some reject this part of life and so cut themselves off from an important internal resource.

One good man that I know described seeking externals as an offense to God, since externals are idols. Since God has seen fit to and desires to make his home in us, it would make sense that he desires us to live from the inside, where he is there ready to guide us, in our spirit.

So, when we disregard our spirit or we look to outside resources to direct us, we are rejecting his presence. The externally referenced person will seek external counterfeits to fulfill or complete those seemingly empty places in his soul.

⟶ **Remember to Check In.**

As we talked about in Part One, counterfeits are those things we think will make us feel better about life, but always come up short, leaving us with shame and other consequences.

Many people call this spiritual concept idolatry, exchanging a thing in my life for the true Source of life. It is taking the gift that comes from the gift-giver and making the gift the source of life. We then forget that the one who gave the gift is the real Source. Often people will seek to hear from God through spiritual processes; prayer, meditation, listening. Many think the voice will be an audible, "This is God!" Sometimes this may happen, but usually this intuitive process results in the "still, small voice", a word picture or faint idea.

Most people believe that we are connected to something greater in the realm of the spirit. For Christians this is called the Holy Spirit. There is strong interaction with the Holy Spirit and our heart. The Holy Spirit relates to us through our internal processes in profound ways to give us guidance, comfort and at times a kick in the butt to move on the right path.

If we listen often, we will usually hear something. Some will claim it is God, others say it is just your intuitive processes. Whatever it is, spirit is another grand resource we must get to know.

How have you been able to listen to your spiritual process?

What are some ways your spirit has guided you in your life?

How could you become more open to listening to spiritual aspects of life?

Soul – "That Which Doesn't Move"

The Soul is different from the Heart in that it stays firm and immovable. Where the Heart moves with emotion, intuitive and spirit, the Soul is a rock in the storms of life.

The Soul of a man is his deep self or identity. It is his ability to choose, decide or just to be. It is the substance or "gravitas" that a man has in life. It is the "weight" your identity and purpose carries. There are people you have encountered in life that seem to be solid, like nothing will faze them or cause them to crumble.

They have a strong sense of who they are and carry themselves with confidence. They have a kind of presence that fills the room or influences everybody in the room. It is the way a musician expresses himself in his music, any craftsman creating with his tools or how a writer can create through his words.

The depth of his being is engaged within the moment, it is not just his mastery, it is his Soul. This is "gravitas", there is gravity in his presence. Years ago, the word gravitas became part of the popular vocabulary during one of the presidential campaigns.

It was a word that described the presence (or lack thereof) of the candidates. Did this man have substance or was he full of fluff? Is he a leader? Did he have Soul was the question.

Your Soul has to do with your identity, your sense of personal value or worthiness, your presence and your confidence. It asks, "of what kind of material are you made?"

Here are the parts of the Soul, the parts of you which stay solid and are not moved.

Identity; Personality, Personal Value or Worthiness, Confidence, Masculinity

Intention/Volition; Will, Choice, Common Sense, Discernment, Decision Making

Purpose; Calling, Interests, Pursuits, Vocation

Motivation; Drive, Priorities, Initiative,

Character; Moral Compass, Discipline, Values, Conscience, Boundaries

Integrity; Integration, Wholeness, Internal Structure

Identity

Your identity is another powerful part of your heart. Your identity is the distinguishing character and personality which makes you who you are and is different from any one else on the planet. Your identity holds your story and all your experiences. It is where your personal value and worthiness rest. Your identity is your true name or your true self, who you really are at your core.

When we are internally referenced, we are able to move in freedom with our true self leading the way. When our identity is referenced externally, we believe what others say about us and then live with those external expectations or narrative. An externally referenced identity is a dead-end where we lose our self.

An internally referenced identity resolves the problems expressed in Part One that had to do with our identity being "reflected" or validated from external sources. The goal is to have an internally validated self where the unsettled questions about being good enough or acceptable are resolved.

With a solid identity, there is no longer a need to engage in comparison, perfectionism or proving yourself through accomplishments. Internal reference results in a solid sense of self.

What we believe about ourselves is our narrative, or the story about who we think we are. We all have a narrative which speaks constantly to us about who we are. This narrative is how we interpret the meaning of all our experiences in light of identity. The narrative that you believe determines our path through life.

You've been told true and false things about who you are from people around you. The Solid Man Process will challenge your false narratives then discover and claim your true narrative. False narratives are those interpretations about your identity that are wrong. To get strong, you must reject the false narratives that you've carried your entire life. Not until you remove the false narrative and embrace the true narrative will you be able to trust your internal resources.

You have character and personality. Your competencies, weaknesses, humor, ways of interacting, ways of energizing, experiences, desires, passion, patterns, story, wounds, accomplishments all come together to define who you really are.

Understanding yourself is absolutely essential to gaining mastery in your life. You must know who you truly are and begin to live fully from your true internal identity. This internal resource guides you from the core of who you are and what is important to you.

Your value and worthiness rests within you, in your being, it is a gift. Whenever we try to find it outside of us in our accomplishments or what others think, our value falters and is distorted. Discovering your true identity and allowing it to guide you through life as a strong internal resource is how the internally referenced life is lived.

➔ **You must find your true self.**

When you engage in finding your true self, shame often comes to life or becomes obvious. We believe that something is wrong with us and that belief holds us back into a fearful posture in life. It keeps us from feeling free enough to live life fully.

Some people soar from early on as though they know a secret. They know what they want in life in High School (or earlier) and then accomplish great things off the starting line. The vast majority of us seem to struggle for years, if not decades, before we start to move with intention.

This struggle is about developing a strong sense of self and what Dr. Brené Brown calls "shame resilience". Some people have a strong sense of self and powerful shame resilience, often from how they were parented. However, like a farmer in rough country, most of us have to claw, scratch and sweat for a good, solid sense of self which is free of toxic shame.

It is hard work to build a self with strong shame resilience. This is what Awakening the Internals is all about, building your inner self with a strong, internally referenced core. When your identity is solid in this way, you will face shame with grace and courage. You will build a new narrative that is based in truth.

⊸ **You must find your true narrative.**

Another significant part of your identity that drives you as an internal resource is your purpose. Your purpose is the reason you exist, what you have been put on the planet for or what you are here to accomplish.

Your purpose is discovered by listening to your passions, desires and identity. It is found by seeking things that make your heart come alive. We will have time later in the process to discover more about your purpose, but for now, know that your purpose is a big part of how your identity drives your life internally.

Knowing who you really are and building a strong, true narrative of your life is essential in the process of awakening your internals.

In what ways have you been disconnected from your true self? How would your life look if your true self ran the show?

We usually don't think of our Identity as a guide to what we do or choose to do in life, how can you follow your Identity into wisdom?

What messages have you received about your identity, that were just plain lies? How could you move forward with a new narrative?

Will

A significant part of our internal processes is to funnel all your good internal information to make good, wise decisions. Intentional decisions come from your wisdom as your mind processes your Internal Resources to determine the best action for the best outcome.

To live an integrated and intentional life you must choose everything; what you do, what you eat, what you say, everything. You create the life you want, by choice. Choose what you do, where you set your personal boundaries, what to believe in, how you want your life to go, the works. You have the power to create the life you want, and your choices make that life happen.

You always have a choice with everything. Masculinity, by definition; moves, chooses and leads. Masculinity is action and intent. The masculine decides to do and say the right thing. An internally referenced man moves and chooses from his deep internal realities with Wisdom.

Choosing is the act of the will, it is what I want. Knowing what you want is vital. This must be secure and not something that can change easily willy-nilly. Have an iron will.

Purpose

There are some people who coach others to actually create their purpose. If you want to be this or that, go for it, it is fruit ripe for the picking. The truth is that we can't really create our purpose. It is not something we can make out of nothing. But something is already there, that's what we want to find since it is a gigantic Internal Resource which will guide you as you create your life.

Your purpose is hidden inside of you even as you are reading this. It already exists within you. Your work in this exercise is to begin the process of discovering it. You will find it from a number of important clues. Those clues awaken your understanding of the deep truths of why you were put on this planet.

> ➔ **"The two most important days in your life are the day you are born and the day you find out why."** - Mark Twain.

I am just bringing up the fact that your purpose is a huge Internal Resource. We'll just barely scratch the surface of finding your purpose, but hopefully you will begin to move in the right direction. To get deeper into this process consider some of the resources at the end of this exercise. For now, here are a few of the most important questions you can ask yourself, so you can discover more about you.

What makes your heart come alive?

Consider the things that move you. What makes you excited or gets you anticipating something? What are the things that really gets you going? It could be spending time with certain people. It could be going someplace. It could be doing something. It could be the preparation of doing something or going somewhere. When have you felt most alive?

➔ **Your heart is where your life is found. Let it come alive!**

What has interested me my whole life?

If you look back, you will see certain patterns. What has captured your attention your whole life? What things keep coming up again and again? What comes up every time you have free time to just let your mind wander when you have no pressure or agenda? What is there?

When you were a kid, you may have been enthralled by World War II or the Civil War when you were a kid. You were amazed with geography and cultures. You discovered math equations way before the teacher taught them in class. Things that captured you, you spent time reading way more than you needed to on an assignment. What were some of these things?

You found out how things work and tore stuff apart to see what was inside. You explored under the house to see how it was built. You wanted to find out what made animals tick. You made everything a game for competition. You read voraciously, or you read nothing at all trying to experience it all. What was your unique interest? As a man you see how you do things the same way as when you were a boy.

How do I do things, every time I have do things?

Think about how you do things like the way you do them. You may be a conformist and do it the same as everyone else. You may be an anti-conformist and do it differently. You may be innovative and do it in a new way. You may be a pragmatist and do it in the easiest or most efficient way.

Every one of us have our own style of getting things done. Some of us focus on the task at hand. Some of us are more interested with the people we are doing it with. Some of us need to make whatever we are doing, fun.

What about getting into the deep details of something or just concerned about the big picture. Knowing how you do things is a big part of discovering your purpose.

What seems to drive or motivate you?

You may be unaware of some of your deeper drivers or motivators in your life. They often stay quite hidden until we look deeper, or like looking for a timid animal, you must wait quietly for it to come forward. Or some of them are bold like crows or roosters making themselves known and in your face.

As we saw in some of the initial Solid Man material, your drivers can be externally referenced. This is a significant thing to observe. Notice if things that are driving you are things like expectations or what might make others approve of you. To discover your true mission, you'll need to find it from your internal resources. So, notice if it is external and reboot.

What moves you to do things or accomplish things? What are you driven to do? I have a friend who later in life began to have a drive to climb all the highest peaks on each continent. His drive took him around the world and in the best shape of his life. Another man, a retired engineer, was compelled to build a business which made it easier to purify water for drinking, and then made it available to people who needed it.

Often, these drives seem to be way out of the box and not ordinary. Sometimes they seem very risky. Sometimes they seem boring and not so exciting. That does not matter. What matters is finding the thing that moves you to action and to making a difference in the world. Asking these questions is the way that you gather good information from this great Internal Resource.

What are some things that might be or have been your purpose?

Motivation

Motivation is a big part of our soul. It is our drive and our initiative. It comes out of our wants and desire. We can be motivated by so much; fear, wants, hopes, obstacles, dreams, visions, core responsibilities, so much.

Our priorities are developed from all these parts of us. Pay attention to what drives you and what pushes you to go, want or pursue anything. Priorities are the things we value and have set ahead of things we don't as much. Our priorities will guide us in decision making and when we choose between different things we want. Have your priorities set in advance, so you can choose from what you want.

Character

Your character is the deep part of your being. It is the qualities that define who you are in your morality, discipline and mental capabilities. Your character rests in your moral compass, self-discipline, your values, and what affects your conscience. We will talk more about that shortly. Your character is developed in your personal boundaries, your actions and ability to use your voice to speak your truth.

Your character is one of the most powerful parts of you when the chips are down, when the shit hits the fan what will you do? A man with moral character already has things implanted within him with immovable character that will guide through difficult or sticky situations. If an opportunity to do something under the radar comes up (sex with a willing woman, a shady deal, etc.) will your character be solid, or will it crumble? What is your character made of?

Integrity

Earlier you learned that your integrity is having a strong structure, wholeness and integration of your whole being. Integrity is also about values and what you believe is right and good (your moral compass or your conscience). We all have a moral compass, something which guides us to knowledge of right and wrong. The question here is whether your moral compass is internally or externally developed. We all start our lives believing what our parents or peers believe.

> ⮑ **Develop your own internal moral compass**

Where have you developed your thoughts about what good character is or what you believe? How have you developed good values or developed spiritual connections or if that is even important? Where is the foundation of your internal moral compass?

Since we developed our initial beliefs about our values from our parents or reactions to our parents, they really are not our values. We may think we developed them ourselves, but for the most part we took on what we thought was right just to fit in and look right. Some values are yours, but most are from others.

> ⮑ **Remember to Check In.**

Challenge whether your values and beliefs are external and passed on to you from others. Question those deeply entrenched ideas to see if they are truly yours. Your values influence your choices, so to be internally referenced in our choices in life it is essential to choose your values. This is how this internal resource thing is done.

Your values will be found from internal experiences and how things seem to resonate with your heart. You may at times have experienced a significant level of anger or intensity with injustice that happened to you or someone else. You knew things were just not right with a situation.

This is your integrity rising up, speaking to you that something must be said or done to change things. It is at this time that presence and voice is coming alive in you. This is where you'll find the heart of what you value.

➔ **Your values drive your decisions.**

Many men are frozen, passive and silent. Their value of self-protection is stronger than the value of influencing the world for good. You've probably heard the quote, "The surest way for evil to prevail is for good men to do nothing." Masculinity has been designed to be that force for good in our world and it is your core of integrity that will guide you.

Fear must not silence you or keep you frozen. You must prepare yourself for uncomfortable moments. So, when the time comes you can face your fears and move and speak with courage.

Often, we think there are only two options when we are moved to confront or challenge a situation, either withdraw to silence or aggressively challenge. Usually all it takes in a situation is two things, speaking up and being there. You don't have to challenge someone to a fight or throw someone out of the room.

It starts by simply having the nerve to stand up and say, "This is not right" or "Does anyone else think this is not ok?".

Whether it is taking care of yourself or speaking up for someone else, it is highly important to follow your gut and be present in the moment with whatever it says to do or say. The world needs good men who stand when the time comes. Speak up in all situations that seem unjust, big ones and small ones.

➔ **Presence and voice are powerful parts of your integrity.**

Your integrity and conscience will guide you well as you develop your strong values and moral compass. Listening to your compass will become so easy to you that you won't even have to think. You will know what is right at any given time or circumstance.

Your integrity is the solid, immovable force behind your own inner authority. It is what gives your life the form and structure you need to move and develop the life you want. From your integrity you will make wise decisions that will define the direction of your life.

In what ways have you been moved to action or remained frozen when your internals were guiding you to move or speak to a situation?

How can your Integrity become a significant source of wise decisions?

Mind – "That Which Notices"

The Mind is that aspect of a man that considers, notices and reflects. It gives him the ability to think and dream. It is his ability to be mindful, conscious and aware. I said earlier that the Mind works best as the interpreter of what is going on. It notices what all your internal resources are saying and put together a great game plan. The Mind does not work well on its own.

If it is ruminating on its own, trying to figure it out without consultation with intuitive, emotion, or moral compass it will go awry quickly. The Mind is not the boss, just a great servant.

The parts of your Internal Information Gathering System that have to do with the Mind are Intelligence, Imagination, Interpretation, Memory and Consciousness. All of these aspects of the Mind combine to create Mindfulness or Awareness in your life.

Intelligence; Logic, Pre-Frontal Cortex, Understanding

Imagination; Creativity, Worry, Ideas, Vision, Goals

Interpretation; Narrative or the story I am telling myself, World-view, Beliefs,

Memory; Anxiety, Triggers, Your History,

Consciousness; Attention, Focus, Awareness, Time Presence (Past-Present-Future), Awareness of Environment and Surrounding Contexts (Safety, Danger, Systems, Culture), Sub-conscious

Intelligence

Our intelligence is brilliant. Problems arise when we give our thinking processes the top position. When our common sense is coupled with our senses of Logic and Understanding, within the full arsenal of our internal resources we will become stronger and more powerful than we ever imagined.

Intelligence is acquiring and applying knowledge toward wisdom. The idea of building your intelligence is at the center of everything I am talking about with gathering all the information from all your internal resources. This builds your intelligence and gaining all this information builds your ability to live with strength.

We have an amazing Pre-Frontal Cortex that can be aware and awake. This is the part of us that is mindful. Mindfulness builds our intelligence. Mindfulness is what helps us to gather all our information.

True education is what gives us the skills to be able to listen to, gather and then apply all the information that internal resources are providing. Most education is dropping information into your head rather than build your internal abilities to learn from all resources, especially your Internal Resources.

Imagination

Imagination is another beautiful part of our mind. Imagination is the beginning of Creativity. Anything that has been created first was imagined. Michelangelo's David was first imagined in the stone. Middle Earth was first imagined by Tolkein. Imagination sometimes is ridiculed as spacing out or lack of focus. Sure, I may not be focusing on what a teacher wants me to focus on, but my good mind is going where it wants to go, into my imagination.

As well as creating, imagination also has the ability to worry about the worst-case scenario that is possible. As our fears are exposed in our worry, this gives us significant information as well. This is true of our hopes as well. We must be aware of whatever it is, and gather that good information about fears, hopes or obstacles.

Imagination also gives me information about vision or dreams. Any entrepreneur must imagine the goals that must be accomplished to build a business that does not exist. You must see it in your imagination with vision, so you can make it happen. Curiosity is another part of our imagination. Curiosity is wondering what is going on or what is happening. Curiosity is the root of science and gathering good information.

Interpretation

Interpretation is how we explain meanings of things. It has been called "The story I am telling myself." This story is important to see and identify. Knowing how we interpret things is essential to be able to gain clarity and not get hung up on false narratives or assessments of what is going on.

Interpretation is the Narrative or World-view of how I see or explain the world around me. It is how we develop our Beliefs. Attention to how you create the narratives in your life is essential to doing this internally referenced stuff well. It is worth your while to identify your own pre-conceived ideas about life and let yourself question those, the world is rarely just as you perceive.

⮩ **Question everything.**

Memory

Your memory is also resting in your mind. Your personal history is an account of your life, experiences, wounds, victories and accomplishments. All your anxieties, fears, triggers, and worries come out of what you remember about your life experiences. Your memory also holds your very positive experiences. Your memory is another strong part the internal resources of your mind.

Consciousness

Whether you call it mindfulness, attention, focus, awareness or consciousness it is all the same thing. It is just being aware of your internal processes and your surroundings. It is actively gaining awareness of time, presence, of environment and surrounding contexts. It is gaining knowledge of safety, danger, of systems around you and how your culture shapes things. Consciousness is another powerful aspect of our mind. Remember all the great parts of your mind.

⮩ **Remember to Check In.**

Strength – "That Which Has Power"

Strength is that aspect of a man that is his power or ability to get things done. It is his influence, legacy and presence. In this category Strength is seen as an over-arching concept which includes any part of a man that has power, influence and capability. As you become more competent you're your life you will move into mastery and mastery will result in Strength. Often, we think of a man's strength with his body or muscles, but there is so much more.

Authority; Mastery, Skill, Competence, Command

Influence; Voice, Presence, Leadership, Collaboration,

Body; Instinctive, Senses, Nerves, Muscles, Physical Well-being, Amygdala (Fight-Freeze-Flee)

Sexuality, Sexual Energy, Sex Drive, Relational Connection, Intimacy, Vulnerability, Reproduction

Energy; Pace, Capability, Skill, Power, Masculinity, Confidence

Frame; Posture, Physical Presence, Courage, Masculinity

Authority

Externally referenced men follow someone else's authority. Rather than following their own self control and decision making, they submit themselves under another person's leadership and influence. Authority as an Internal Resource is essentially asking yourself, "What do I want?".

It is just having a sense of what you want and leading your own life in the direction you want it to go. It is trusting yourself that you have some good ideas about what some great things would be to do. This is under the heading of Strength since taking control of his own life and developing his abilities moves a man through these stages; Skill, Competence, Mastery, Creating and then Command.

As you grow in competence you will move toward power and eventually you will take "command" of whatever you are doing. You will become and influencer, rather than the influenced. You will become the leader rather than the follower. You will become a master of your life rather than just a student. All this by listening to your Internal Resources.

Body

Many people view the body with disdain, as less important or even bad. The body is very important to your internal process. It is not a lesser part of you. Since the body is a vital part of your system, it is important to nurture your body with good nutrition, sleep, exercise, healthcare and affection. It is a brilliant part of your internal system with so much to offer.

The body is not just some container like Tupperware ™ holding all your being together. It is a brilliant part of your internal system with so much to offer. The body gives you amazing vital information in real time that guides you well. You have probably experienced things like tingling on the back of your neck, cottonmouth, or butterflies before giving a speech. This is the type of information the body throws out there to remind you to stop for a moment to breathe. We have lost the fine art of listening to our body.

➔ The body is a rich wellspring of internal information.

Our sexual energy, posture, chemistry, tension, reactions, muscle memory or "fight/flight mechanism" all teach us who we are and what is happening around us. Physical signals like muscle tightness, headaches, sweaty palms, breathing changes, heart rate, or tingling, is your body telling you about your state of being and what you may need to do in order to thrive. What is this anxiety I feel? Why are my shoulders slumping? Wow, my breathing is shallow, what's that?

Your body runs on an instinctive level. The instinctive is not about intuitively knowing something; instinctive is about knowing how to do something. It's like a Border collie that herds kids around the yard even though it's never been around sheep.

Animals move in such a way that you know there is something guiding them on a physical or DNA level. They don't have to stop and think about what is acceptable or right, they just do what they were designed to do. The same is true for us, when we think too much, we often miss our opportunity.

The instinctive guides in the development of essential aspects of life like self-care, sexuality, protecting, and providing. Your body is full of Wisdom, learn how to listen to it. Our muscles, nerves, organs, senses, all of our body parts and chemistry come together to notify us of some of the most important information for living well. Our physical well-being is a primary tool for full living.

It is like a well-timed joke with a group of friends. Good humor just shows up randomly in conversations. If you filter it by asking yourself if it will be funny or how well it will be received, you'll miss the chance and it will fall flat. But if you let it out there with your internal timing, it could be very funny.

There are things we know how to do, even if we have never done it. Our bodies have a way of guiding us if we let it. The instinctive guides in the development of essential aspects of life like self-care, sexuality, protecting, and providing.

⮒ **Your body is full of Wisdom, learn how to listen to it.**

Athletics is actually just the harnessing of the instinctive for a fun, competitive experience. Even though the instinctive is not designed to run the show, it is a significant source of information. Following your instincts adds some very fun and playful opportunities in life.

In order to live full, free lives we will need to discover the depth of our physical being and listen for the cues the body is constantly sending out.

How could you hear the instinctive information your body gives you?

How has your body spoken to you and how could you start to listen more fully to your body?

Energy

Your energy is another important part of your physical being. Energy is that part of us that has power to get things done. Sometimes you are exhausted or sometimes you are ready to get going. This is your energy level. It is important to pay attention to this so you can care for yourself by getting rest or food. Listening to your body is essential in order to thrive.

Your energy often is represented as emotional energy. Somehow it physically rises up in us or shows up in unique ways for each person. Your emotional energy always is connected to your body. When you become proficient at listening to your body, you will become a master of your emotions. Our energy is represented by our pace of life and the timing of how we move. Some of us drive and do. Some of us have a relaxed mode.

We may have margins of space or we may run a tight methodology. Our internal capabilities, skills and abilities is another way our physical body energy is expressed in life. Knowing our inherent abilities and skill-set is prime evidence of our internal power and leadership expression. Confidence is our ability to be self-assured in your internal value, competence and being.

Sexuality

Our sexuality is another beautiful part of our physical being. Awareness of sexual cues like arousal, interest, or desire is important so you can follow the guidance of your physical being to what you want in life. It is part of our Strength since it encompasses so many different parts of our being; body, desire, love, procreation, and spirit. Sexuality has historically been a point of contention for many people as though it is wild and out of control.

It is true that people without much integrity or self-control experience much folly in this area of life, but that does not mean that our sexuality is to be avoided or seen as sinful. Many traditions focus on restraining sexuality and since Sexuality is a very valuable part of you that is usually relegated to the basement, it cannot be put down there, it is a prime aspect of your body. Releasing sexuality does not mean to just let it rip without consideration of Wisdom or without your moral compass; it is allowing it a position at the table with the rest of your internal resources.

Our sex drive is powerful as a part of our Strength. Yes, it needs to be under the influence of Wisdom, but it needs to be set free at times as well. Sexuality is one of your most valuable asset.

➔ **Sexuality is the Great Connector.**

Sexuality guides people into human connection and intimacy like nothing else. Sex is the great connector. Since connection and closeness is a primary human need, sexuality provides that beautifully. Sexuality creates connection and is life-giving in many ways.

Our sexuality is a place of vulnerability where we can truly allow ourselves to be seen. Being naked with someone else opens us up to the most profound vulnerable experiences of life. Yes, we may be physically seen, but our sexuality allows our full self to be revealed.

Often this feels very awkward and clumsy, but it is the path to intimacy. It is one of the greatest avenues of legacy in our lives as well. Sex is very much about procreation and continuing the species.

Our children are a significant way we can leave our mark on the world. To fully embrace ourselves, we must embrace our sexuality. In order to live full, free lives we will need to discover the depth of our physical being and listen for the cues the body is constantly sending out.

Sexuality can be a difficult aspect of life for many people with abusive or difficult experiences. There are many people who experience sexual struggles often characterized as "Sex Addiction". Sexuality is often a place where shame thrives. This is all true, but it in no way diminishes the value and depth that our sexuality has been designed to bring to our lives.

> ➔ **To fully embrace ourselves, we must embrace our sexuality.**

For many men, sexuality is a significant place of shame. Because of this, some men pray diligently that God would take it away from them. It is as though sexuality is some kind of parasite that sucks your life away and keeps you locked into sinful behavior. This belief is tough to beat, but as you begin to embrace your sexuality, you will begin to experience the greatness for which it was intended.

Presence

Presence is about you being here, now. Presence is being awake, aware and conscious of your surroundings and of your internal workings. Presence is influence and creativity, leading your life and making a difference in your present environment. Presence is relational connection and purposeful interaction with others in real time.

It may sound odd that I am including this concept as an internal resource of the heart. Think of presence as something that you own, as in "My Presence".

Think of it as something that is part of your life. You carry your Presence with you. People notice your Presence when you enter into a room. Up to this point your Presence may not have had a huge impact on the room, but the more you are aware of your Presence, the more it will build influence.

Often men will live life like a chess game, thinking three or more moves ahead. While this works for chess, it keeps you out of the game in real life. Maintaining Presence requires staying in the moment with whatever your internal resources are giving you. This will take practice, but the more you do stay with yourself, the better you'll get at listening to your internal voice.

> ➔ *Remember to check in with yourself, often.*

Presence has to do with time and space. Presence requires that you are aware of the "present" and are in the "now". If you are lost in worry or anxiety of the future or holding regret, shame or resentment from the past, you will not be present. Your head will be in the sand. When this happens, you will go into "auto pilot" and not be conscious of what is happening inside you, let alone outside of you.

Men sometimes will get locked into a pattern of compartmentalizing where they will be in the zone only focused on one thing. Often this results in disregarding important parts of life. When I experience true presence in my own life, I begin to actually drive my own life. I am the one who determines the pace and balance through my own inner authority. I am able to influence my life through creating the life that works great for me.

➔ **I make things happen because I am here.**

Just because Presence is not tangible, or concrete does not mean it is not rich with vital information for living fully. The feedback you receive from present interactions is what you're looking for from this prime internal resource.

Presence is about influence; the ability to make changes to your environment or in the lives of other people. Influence exists only when you are present. It is setting your own personal pace and creating the life you want. Presence is leading your own life and making what you desire happen. Most women long for a man who is present.

➔ **Presence is the interface between you, here and now.**

Presence is intention. Intention is the posture of leadership. Leadership is an intentional posture of knowing what you want and then making that happen. Intention is action which is developed from the core of what a man wants to accomplish as he influences and creates the life he wants. Intention is choice, power and action.

Presence is confidence or being wherever you are with your full self. Confidence is trust and reliance in your own power and abilities. Confidence allows you to be fully engaged with people and whatever your surroundings bring. When you know that you have what it takes to handle just about any situation that comes your way, you can engage the present with confidence.

Many men have a horrible habit of withdrawing or disengaging from present moments, especially when things get tense or difficult. You must fight this urge.

To be alive and engaged you must stay present in every moment, difficult or not.

To develop confidence, you will need to listen and embrace all the information that comes your way as you interact with present circumstances. Grow in your awareness of the present and gain insight from every present moment.

Presence is expressed in your posture. This will be a significant way for you to recognize and observe how you are engaging with your world. Notice when you are confident in your posture. See when you are closed or when you are engaged. Notice how your physical posture reflects your presence and engagement with your surroundings. Your Presence is a powerful part of your being.

What could you do to live more in the "Now"?

Influence

While our Presence is a huge part of our power as a man, it is only part of our Influence. Our Influence is how our power is expressed in our world. As with any internal resource it is important to build awareness of how this internal aspect of your being exists within you and interacts with the world around you.

Your influence is expressed in your abilities and skills, in your physical presence, in your confident presence, and in how you create spaces of safety and collaboration. Leadership is the ability to influence. Leadership is a huge way that your influence plays itself out in the world. Your Voice is one of the most powerful influencers in your internal resource repertoire. The most powerful part of a man is his Voice. And as we age it is important to understand the transition of masculine power from muscular presence to Voice.

You must prepare yourself for uncomfortable moments. So, when the time comes you can face your fears and move and speak with courage. Usually all it takes in a situation is two things, speaking up and being there. Whether it is taking care of yourself or speaking up for someone else, it is highly important to follow your gut and be present in the moment with whatever it says to do or say. The world needs good men who speak up.

How could you increase the influence you have in your own life?

Frame

Like Integrity, Frame is having a strong structure, wholeness and integration of your whole being. Frame is that sense that you have a solid core in your beliefs, identity and character. It is the thing that holds fast in relationship in tension or conflict. Integrity is also about values and what you believe is right and good (your moral compass or your conscience).

We all have a moral compass, something which guides us to knowledge of right and wrong. The question here is whether your moral compass is internally or externally developed. Your integrity and conscience will guide you well as you develop your strong values and moral compass.

Listening to your compass will become so easy to you that you won't even have to think. You will know what is right at any given time or circumstance. Your integrity is the solid, immovable force behind your own inner authority. It is what gives your life the form and structure you need to move and develop the life you want. From your integrity you will make strong, wise decisions that will define the direction of your life.

Internal Frame is a powerful part of a man. It is where his strength is derived. We've talked about all the parts that create Strength, bringing them all together in a beautiful machine is what Frame is. It is all the parts creating a structure of strength and influence.

As you will learn in Pillar Four, Solid Frame is one of the Foundational principles of Masculinity, it is what is part of our definition as a man. Bring all your avenues of Strength together in all its glory!

In what ways does your Frame crumble or tilt? How could you build it stronger?

External Law / Responsibilities - "That Which is Chosen"

This section refers to any external category that you have chosen to become an internal reality. It is something that you have taken as a truth, a personal discipline, restraint or just general wisdom that you believe that will guide you toward wise living. These could be the laws of nature or the land. They could be choices to be a father or a student. They could be matters of faith and who I will choose to follow in life. These are also categories you may not have chosen but are now part of your life like health issues, relational problems, or Family of Origin.

These laws and responsibilities are part of our Internal Resources in that they are aspects of life either chosen or given which must be accepted for what they are and then taken into account as we pursue wisdom and wise action. These external things which have been made internal are our link to the external world. We are not totally an island and so therefore we must consider all the ways we are linked to the world and the choices we have in that interaction.

Laws

Natural Law is the first category of laws that we live under. These are things that like time, gravity or weather. This also includes the fact that we have restraints of distance where we need to take time to walk, drive or fly places. It is our physical health as we can only do so much as our bodies are limited. Not that we choose that these laws exist, but we must choose to place ourselves under them. The choice comes as we choose not to experience natural consequences by jumping off a cliff or driving into an abutment.

Moral Law is also a choice we make since there are consequences here as well. These ideas are what forms our sense of right and wrong, of what is just, what is wise and what makes sense. It is our values that we have chosen to make our own. It is what rules or codes we have chosen to live by. We all have these, what is important is that we consciously choose them.

Civil Law are the restrictions that the local, state or federal government has placed upon the people of its jurisdiction. These are the traffic Laws, domestic laws, contracts, limits in behavior (violence, aggression, abuse, etc.), money, taxes and thing like that. Here it is our choice to vote for certain people, try to make changes in the laws or to move to a new place that better fits us. This choice is like the fact that every time a new President is voted in, people threaten to move to Canada.

Religious Law are very specific laws that we chose to follow because of our belief system. There are tons of faiths and denominations one may place themselves under. All these could include things like following the 10 commandments, experiencing different traditions or behaviors like fasting, prayer, tithing, service attendance, community service, feasts or wearing certain items of clothing. These we have taken in as an Internal Resource to guide us toward wise living or lifestyle we seek.

Responsibilities

Marriage is a significant responsibilities people choose. It is making a covenant with one woman. It requires negotiating needs/wants, conflicts, and well-being. When you choose to be married your life changes because you now have a completely new set of internal boundaries and priorities you did not have as a single person. You have chosen to be responsible for another person.

One of the responsibilities we choose is family. Family includes taking care of kids, not getting enough sleep, and making sure everyone's health is ok. It is ensuring all are being educated from pre-school to college. It is choosing that your resources are going to domestic upkeep, protection and providing. Along with sleep deprivation, you are choosing time limitations, money limitations and energy limitations. But you are also choosing one of the most fulfilling endeavors a human can choose. It is a choice, and it becomes a powerful Internal Resource.

Another responsibility we choose is work. We choose how much we work, our commitment to a certain company, to submit to a certain boss, or to be self-employed. We choose where and when to build or abilities and competencies in this field or that. We choose the jobs that have the perks we want, whether vacation or sick days, bonuses or salaries, insurance or retirement plans, we choose what we want and this choice also dictates our choices in life.

We choose the restriction that school brings us. The classwork, class time, submission to teacher's whims, submission to school's requirements are all things we choose when we choose to become more educated or pursue certifications or a new career. During these seasons of life, we place ourselves in situations that we must consider as we choose and choices like this have strong implications as we listen to our Internal Resources.

We also have various limitations we may not have chosen, but we must accept as realities as we learn to choose and live. Things like physical needs (food, air, water, etc.), physical problems (hearing/sight loss, IBS, arthritis, etc.), mental health (any diagnosis like OCD, Bipolar, etc.), intelligence, wealth, ugliness, weight, upbringing, racism are all possible limitations in our lives that affect how we choose and move.

Other possibilities in this category are when we choose certain disciplines or restraints like eating well, exercising, any moratorium we might choose to overcome an addiction or spiritual disciplines. We may listen to wise people or mentors who will give us good insight to living.

Listening to these wise people will help gain understanding about life through podcasts, books or coaching. Regardless how we do it, these are all things we choose to become internal realities to guide us toward Wisdom.

Dark Side - "That Which is Hidden"

The Dark Side is the conglomeration of all those aspects of your life that don't seem to be ok and not the best parts of you. It's the darkness or aspects of you that can be mean, ugly or just plain wrong. It's those bad decisions that come from a place in you that is afraid or controlling. It's what comes out when you are self-protective, forgetful or living in scarcity.

These are what you do when you are uncertain with fear. It is your history of wounds, trauma and the pain you have experienced. The Dark Side is the things you are or have been addicted to or what is commonly called your "Drug of Choice", which could be anything. It is the mistakes and embarrassments you have had in your life.

This Dark Side stuff is the shame you have held and all secrets you hold. They are limitations that you refuse to acknowledge. It is your Shadow Self and how it shows up. It is the Void with all its emptiness and possibility of death.

We need to be able to address these parts of us as real and part of the process of listening to your Internal Resources. Especially because we know these things are all floating around down inside us beneath the surface. If we disregard them, we will miss some really good in formation, even if it is tough to observe these things inside of you.

Denying that anything dark is there or resisting the thing usually just hides it and then it has a way of creeping in somewhere with negative influence. To include it in your pursuit of Wisdom, just call it out, name it and let it be part of the decision process.

For instance, it would be recognizing that there is something inside of you that wants to have sex with a hot co-worker or to steer into oncoming traffic or to scream at a referee at your kid's t-ball game or that you feel really insecure about your job. Just noticing and owning the fact that something is there is a huge part of the battle; observe it and call it out.

So, when you allow any of the Dark Side stuff into the decision-making funnel, it is not so that it has a huge influence, but to allow yourself to see it, challenge it and then make the wisest decision. You may want to have sex with the co-worker, but you know what wisdom would say, "All desires are not meant to be fulfilled." Just recognize that it is part of you and make wise choices.

Here is a list of possible Dark Side categories.

Difficult Story Themes; Wounds, Trauma, Abuse, Losses/Grief, Lost Dreams, Abandonment, Alienation, Rejections, Unfulfilled Quests, Humiliations, Hard knocks, Counterfeits/Addictions, Lies I have Believed, Mistakes, Regrets, Foolishness, Failures, Near Misses, Consequences, Penalties, Unexamined Stuff, Hidden Secrets, Forgetting who you are, Uncertainty; Fears, Anxiety, Insecurities, Taboos, Shame, Distortions, Meaninglessness, Boredom, Self-Doubt, Doubts, Questions, Ambiguity, Confusion, Unanswered Questions, Chaos; Mystery, The Unknown, Out of Control, Desire to Control or Manage, Attachment to Outcome, Panic, No Boundaries, Discomfort, Exposure to Fear, Things that really Stretch me, Limitations; Disabilities, Challenges, Weaknesses, Enemies, Disease, Privilege, Prejudices, Restrictions, Mental Illness, Chemical Imbalances, Family of Origin Crap, Inner "Demons"; Shadow Self, Violence, Abusive Tendencies, Monstrous Capabilities, Evil Thoughts, Immoral Ideas/Desires, Lusts, Ruminating Thoughts, Compulsivity, Impulsivity, Neediness, Need for Validation, Reactivity, Feeling like a Fraud, Fantasies, Void; Emptiness, Death, Desert, Wilderness, Dark Night of the Soul, Obstacles, Excuses are just a few things that could be included in the Dark Side for consideration.

The Decision-Making Funnel

The final step with internal processes is to funnel all your good internal information to make good, wise decisions. Intentional decisions come from your Wisdom as your mind processes your Internal Resources to determine the best action for the best outcome.

To live an integrated and intentional life you must choose everything; what you do, what you eat, what you say, everything. You create the life you want, by choice. Choose what you do, where you set your personal boundaries, what to believe in, how you want your life to go, the works. You have the power to create the life you want, and your choices make that life happen.

➔ **You always have a choice with everything.**

Externally referenced men have a difficult time with choice. The word "decide" explains some of this angst. I am not sure where he heard this, but my friend Danny Ballard pointed out to me that "Decide" ends with "-cide" the same as suicide or genocide. When you de-cide something dies. All the other options die.

When I decide to choose one woman, my options with other women die. I choose one career path and for now other career options die.

⊙ **Life is uncertain, therefore deciding requires courage.**

Masculinity, by definition; moves, chooses and leads. Masculinity is action and intent. The masculine decides to do and say the right thing. A man chooses and lives with his decisions with strength and honor. An internally referenced man moves and chooses from his deep internal realities with wisdom.

Our goal is to be integrated where all our internal resources are working together to guide us into wisdom. But often life will bring times of confusion and uncertainty. Sometimes we will experience a "Shame Grenade" which dis-integrates and blows all our resources away so we cannot hear them. You know the feeling when you are giving a speech and you stumble with your words or something happens; you get cottonmouth, you stammer and entirely forget what you were going to say, that's dis-integration. You no longer have access to anything, and you lock up. When this happens, you must just gather your resources back. Just take a breath, ask for a drink, take a timeout and then check-in and remember, "I've got this."

Choosing answers the questions, "Where am I going?" or "What do I want to accomplish?" "What is the best thing to do or say right now?" A man does life on purpose. Most of us have lost connection with our ability to choose and lead, because we have lost touch with what we want. We are more concerned with pleasing others; what does my boss want, what would make my wife happy or what is expected of me?

⊙ **You are responsible for your sense of well-being.**

During the decision-making process it is especially important to be aware of the Shadow Self. The Shadow Self will try to hi-jack your decisions. You will end up making decisions out of fear or confusion. Take your time, build awareness and attend to whatever it is you are afraid of or confused about. The more you recognize the Shadow Self, the less it will interfere.

☞ **There are always two options: do the right thing or say the right thing.**

The two most powerful parts of a man come from these two moves; Presence and Voice. When we are externally referenced, we have no choice. We have no will. We have no intent. Procrastination takes over and we lose our personal power. Being a powerful man requires being present and speaking clearly.

Choosing requires that I know what I want. Externally referenced people don't even ask themselves, "What do I want?" To live from the inside-out you must know what you want. When you begin to choose you will finally be able to lead your own life in freedom.

☞ **Listen to your Internal Resources and you will find Wisdom.**

Freedom is the "End Game" with the Solid Man Process and the ultimate goal of the internally referenced life. As a masculine virtue, freedom is essential in the life of every man. Freedom is the ability to act freely, doing and living as you want, without undue restraints or restrictions.

Freedom is creating the life you want, leading your own life and expanding into multiple arenas of presence.

Choosing is the expression of freedom and will keep you on the road of the internally referenced life. Every choice comes from an internal process of asking yourself what you want or what is right. It requires awareness and consciousness of what is happening in your internal world. It requires that you are in touch with your identity, emotions, desires, well-being and interaction with your environment.

☞ **You always have a choice.**

<u>**Choice Directive –**</u>

Listen and gather wisdom from your core resources, then choose your best course of action with wisdom and courage.

How have you been reluctant to make decisions?

What would help you have more courage to choose?

How could you become more responsible for choosing your own sense of well-being?

What is your plan to become proficient at mastering the art of living from the inside-out? List five things you could do today to begin living inside-out?

Internal Resource Chapter Overview

Awakening your internal life is the pathway into personal freedom. Freedom is developed as a man moves from being enslaved to the expectations of others to living from a life of listening to and moving from his internal core.

The internally referenced life exists when a person is defined and driven from the internal resources that exist within that person's being or core. The definition (value, worthiness and acceptance) of the person comes from the truth about who he is as an individual with precise characteristics and personality.

Dignity and value exist for every person and worthiness exists inherently in every man. The drivers or motivation comes from the good internal resources that are designed to guide and lead as a man moves through life.

Internals guide a man well as he creates good, wise choices in life. This is what Wisdom is all about, making good choices so everyone can thrive. Wisdom is seeking the best possible outcome in life. A man's Internal Resources guide him to those good choices.

All the components of a man's heart are there for him to listen to and to follow in real time presence. The challenge is to get good at listening and accessing all the good resources within you. You do not need to be externally referenced. You have all you need inside. True, listen and observe what is going on outside. Gather good Wisdom from outside, but take that all into your Internal Resource reservoir to use any time you need it.

⮑ **Your Internal Resources will always guide you well.**

Overview of Internal Resource Concepts

Outcomes and Goals
Primary Outcomes – Wisdom (Optimum Judgment for Optimum Action), Freedom (Unapologetically being who I am and moving with intention) and Mastery (being good at being a man)

Secondary Outcomes – Healthy Relationships, Valuable Experiences, Safe Environment, Expansive Lifestyle, Influential Leadership, Creating the life you want, Increased Personal Power, Solidness, Masculine Presence, Life Purpose, Life Balance, Full Integration of Self, Confidence
Primary Process Goal – Integration; All of your internal resources working together as one solid unit to provide you with the best information you can receive at any given time.

Primary Process Obstacle – Shame Grenade or Dis-Integration, Perpetual State of Dis-Integration; Where all of your internal resources are blown to bits and you are lost in a mass of confusion and chaos. Either in a perpetual state of disintegration or a short period in which you consciously gather them back one, by one.

Remember the Directives

Shadow Self Directive – Stay conscious and aware of how the Shadow Self comes alive in your life. When it raises its ugly head, notice it and then regroup.

Wisdom Directive – Seek the optimum action for every decision in your life.

Mind Directive – Use your mind to gather information and to discern your optimum action.

Core Directive – Always live with a conscious, open heart from your core, by listening to all of your Internal Resources.

Choice Directive – First listen and gather wisdom from your core resources, then choose your best course of action with wisdom and courage.

All Your Internal Resources

Heart – That Which Moves

Intuitive; Gut, Humor, Instinctive, 6th sense, "Blink"
Passion; Emotions, Desire, Wants, Well-being, Love, Compassion, Empathy, Sacrifice
Spirit; Faith, Beliefs, Worship, Connection w/the Divine or Source, Transcendence
Humor; Laughter, Fun, Enjoyment, Gratitude

Soul – That Which Doesn't Move

Identity; Personality, Personal Value or Worthiness, Confidence, Masculinity
Intention/Volition; Will, Choice, Common Sense, Discernment, Decision Making
Purpose; Calling, Interests, Pursuits, Vocation
Motivation; Drive, Priorities, Initiative,
Character; Moral Compass, Discipline, Values, Conscience, Boundaries
Integrity; Integration, Wholeness, Internal Structure

Mind – That Which Notices
Intelligence; Logic, Pre-Frontal Cortex, Understanding
Imagination; Creativity, Worry, Ideas, Vision, Goals
Interpretation; Narrative or the story I am telling myself, World-view, Beliefs,
Memory; Anxiety, Triggers, Your History,
Consciousness; Attention, Focus, Awareness, Time Presence (Past-Present-Future), Awareness of Environment and Surrounding Contexts (Safety, Danger, Systems, Culture), Sub-conscious

Strength – That Which has Power
Authority; Mastery, Skill, Competence, Command
Influence; Voice, Presence, Leadership, Collaboration,
Body; Instinctive, Senses, Nerves, Muscles, Physical Well-being, Amygdala (Fight-Freeze-Flee)
Sexuality, Sexual Energy, Sex Drive, Relational Connection, Intimacy, Vulnerability, Reproduction
Energy; Pace, Capability, Skill, Power, Masculinity, Confidence
Frame; Posture, Physical Presence, Courage, Masculinity

Laws/Responsibilities – That Which is Chosen
Laws; Natural, Moral, Civil, Religious
Responsibilities; Family, Marriage, Work, School, Limitations

Dark Side – That Which is Hidden
Secrets, Uncertainty, Fears and Self-Protection, Difficult Experiences, Wounds/Traumas, Addictions, Mistakes, Limitations, Shadow Self, The Void

Solid Challenge #10: Remembering

Remembering is a central part of regaining integrity in your life. So often we will go through life on default. We just move without intention or purpose. We often forget and forgetting is a huge problem for a man.

Let that idea sink in. When we forget we lose everything; we lose ourselves, our purpose, and even our life. This exercise is for the purpose of helping you to identify and remember, then keep it in the forefront of your mindfulness throughout everyday of your life.

We need reminders that will regularly and randomly remind us the truth about life, who we are, where we've been and where we want to go.

You'll need to discover things to have in your life that will remind you of what you have learned. We will forget. Remember that the only thing that is wrong with you – is that you forget! So we need all the help we can get to remember.

You could use sticky notes on mirror, a tattoo, rocks in your yard, pictures, a song, a place, your wedding ring, a tree you planted, a certain word, a photo, a movie or story, a piece of jewelry, stacked stones on a trail, a symbol, a picture, a book, a scripture reference, a sticker, a quote, an ornament, a trophy, a certificate, a flag, a golf club, artwork, or an inside joke. Anything can be used to help you remember.

What do you need help remembering?

What will you use to help you remember?

CONCLUSION

In Part One we identified the source of the problems that men face today as an externally referenced life. The externally referenced life exists when a man's identity and worthiness are defined by external categories and when he is driven or motivated by what would make others happy, what others want and what people expect from him.

The difficult outcomes of the externally referenced life are experienced in the lives of many men in our culture today; purposelessness, porn compulsivity, powerlessness, lack of confidence, and confusion about masculinity. As men disregard their internal life, they experience deadness or disruption in their emotional and spiritual lives as well.

The externally referenced life has left us with generations of men who are disconnected from themselves and therefore disconnected from deep relationships. They are unable to provide what their women and the world needs from men.

This is the problem; men all over the world have lost their good, strong presence because of an externally referenced life. It is time to put down your device and listen to your internal resources.

The Solid Man Process is here to reclaim that presence for you and all other men. This process begins with the solution of shifting the reference of your life from external to internal.

Part One Practices:

1) Clarity: Develop clarity with how you have been trained to maintain an externally referenced life. Learn the ways in which this has influenced the decisions and way of living you have developed.

2) Overcome the Lie: Understand how you have believed the lie that you are broken and flawed. Change that.

3) Definers: Identify how you are externally referenced with your identity; who you are, where you find your value or worthiness and what or who defines you.

4) Drivers: Identify how you are externally referenced with your motivation; who drives you, where you find your intentions and to what or whom you are trying to prove yourself.

Part One identified the ways men are externally referenced. Part Two showed the pathway to becoming internally referenced; to awaken your deep internal life by listening to your internal resources.

Remember, awakening your internal life is the pathway into personal freedom. Freedom is developed as a man moves from being enslaved to the expectations of others to living from a life of listening to and moving from his internal core.

The internally referenced life exists when a person is defined and driven from the internal resources that exist within that person's being or core. The definition (value, worthiness and acceptance) of the person comes from the truth about who he is as an individual with precise characteristics and personality.

Dignity and value exists for every person and worthiness exists inherently in every man. The drivers or motivation comes from the good Internal Resources that are designed to guide and lead as a man moves through life.

Internals guide a man well as he creates good, wise choices in life. This is what wisdom is all about; making good choices so everyone can thrive. Wisdom is seeking the best possible outcome in life. A man's Internal Resources guide him to those good choices.

All the components of a man's heart are there for him to listen to and to follow in real time presence. Your internal resources will always guide you well.

Part Two Practices:

1) Remembering: Remember that you have what it takes, you are more than enough. Remember that you are not broken and you can live in freedom.

2) Check-In: Notice what is going on in your world, both external and internal. Check in with yourself, often. Stay awake and conscious.

3) Seek Wisdom: In everything that you do take time to gather wisdom in your life so you can determine the most optimum path in your life. Seek wisdom in everything that you do.

4) Open Heart: Live with an open heart as much as possible. Listen to your Internal Resources as much as you can and allow them to guide your interactions and decisions.

Now, go master the art of living from the inside-out.

Group Presentation Questions; The Solution

What is your plan to become proficient at mastering the art of living from the inside-out?

List five things you could do today to begin living inside-out?

Wisdom is simply Optimum Judgment for Optimum Action; how can you begin to implement the intentional pursuit of wisdom in your life?

In what ways do you get stuck in your head or try to figure it out? Or how has your mind tried to be the boss in your life?

Of the categories; Heart, Soul, Mind and Strength, which is your strongest or weakest?

Of all the categories under these four, which are your favorites and which ones are difficult for you?

Of the Laws and Responsibilities, which have you chosen and how do they impact your decisions?

Of the Dark Side categories, which ones hold the most weight in your life? Which ones have you hidden too much?

How have you been reluctant to make decisions? What would help you have courage to choose?

What internal areas in your life could you become more proficient in?

When do you most commonly feel dis-integrated, when the shame grenade hits and it all falls apart?

Share your most profound insights from this lesson.

Share four intentional changes you could make to move toward being more internally directed.

SOLIDMAN

strong · present · confident

ABOUT THE AUTHOR

Ken Curry is a father, husband, mentor, friend and a Licensed Marriage and Family Therapist (LMFT) in Littleton, Colorado. His specialty is manhood, masculinity and relationships. He is continually exploring new avenues of strength, vitality and purpose for men.

Ken works from the premise that masculinity is good and that each man brings significance into our world. He believes that men have been designed to move with freedom, presence and strength. Along with individual and relationship counseling, Ken provides ongoing groups for men to build personal integrity in order to influence the world with intent and passion.

Ken has been developing the Solid Man Process so men can get their hearts back, develop their solid core, create freedom, grow healthy relationships, develop strength in their personal lives and overcome distracting issues like anger or porn.

 SOLIDMAN.ORG

30334792R00098

Made in the USA
San Bernardino, CA
24 March 2019